The Void Generation

The Void Generation

How a Generation of Void Restraining Orders Voided the Lives of a Generation

by
Conrad Baldwin

Illustrated with the Forms, Reports, and Decisions of the California Judicial Council

Disclaimer and Legal Notices

This book is designed to provide accurate and authoritative information in regard to the subject matter covered as of the date of publication. However, because of the rate at which policies, laws, and rules can change, the author reserves the right to alter and update this book at any time to include any new or different information.

Although every precaution has been taken to insure accuracy in the preparation of this work, the information contained in this book is distributed on an "as is" basis, with no warranty of any kind. Neither the author nor the publisher shall have any liability whatsoever to any person or entity with respect to any loss or damage caused or alleged to be caused directly or indirectly by the information and public documents contained in this book.

This book is sold with the understanding that neither the author nor the publisher is engaged in rendering any legal, accounting, or other professional services. If as a result of the information contained in this book you wish to obtain expert legal, law enforcement, or other professional advice or assistance, you should seek the services of provably honest and competent practitioners.

Copyright © 2014 by Conrad Baldwin

ISBN-10   0-9898283-3-6
ISBN-13   978-0-9898283-3-8

Paperback Edition

Dedication

This book is dedicated to all those who were imprisoned for allegedly violating the firearms prohibition notices that were missing from all of these void forms. Hang in, truth will out.

Acknowledgments

Several legal professionals have reviewed the documents and discussions presented in this book for accuracy, but requested anonymity. That these legally and procedurally knowledgeable contributors are not named does not, however, diminish the influence of their many helpful suggestions nor the author's profound gratitude for their contributions.

Thanks to everyone who helped in the researching and writing of this book, with special thanks to the staff of the San Francisco Law Library. Their patient assistance with the heavy lifting required to search through the library's voluminous archives for relevant back issues of West's California Judicial Council Forms was crucial to both the inception and completion of this investigative work.

Table of Contents

Chapter 1
Introduction

This book is intended as a picture book of key documents that illustrate and explain a series of publishing mistakes made by the Judicial Council of California between 1999 and 2007 and the far reaching consequences of those mistakes for the people of California – as those mistakes are revealed in the Judicial Council's own archives and other public records.

As you read through this book, you will find brief discussions of the significance of each pictured document, along with extracted quotes that focus on the words and phrases you need to fully understand the scope and consequences of this series of Judicial Council publishing mistakes. You can check the accuracy of the extracted quotes by comparing them with the actual wording of the public documents, all of which are reproduced for your comparison on adjacent pages.

The documents in this book are all available from public sources, either online, in Court and government archives, or from the public law library. These public records are the work products of public employees, and as such they are in the public domain, freely available for you or anyone else to copy and share. These documents are also self-authenticating, requiring no proof that they are accurate reproductions beyond the verifiable existence of the originals in the public record.

The public record demonstrates that on January 1, 1999 the Judicial Council published three restraining order forms, the DV-110 (*Order to Show Cause and Temporary Restraining Order*), the DV-130 (*Restraining Order After Hearing*), and the MC-220 (*Protective Order in Criminal Proceeding*), all three of which were Constitutionally *"void for vagueness"* because the Notice Regarding Firearms they contained ambiguously informed respondents the Court had only the indefinite jurisdictional *authority* to order the relinquishment of firearms at a prior noticed hearing. Additionally, the Firearm Restriction notice in two of these restraining order forms, the DV-110 and the DV-130, violated Constitutional due process guarantees by ordering the respondents to relinquish any firearms they owned or possessed before they had an opportunity to appear and be heard in opposition to the firearms surrender order at a noticed hearing in open court.

The public record also demonstrates that on January 1, 2000 the Judicial Council published and in some cases republished eleven (11) mandatory restraining order forms that violated the newly enacted Senate Bill 218 (Solis) (Stats. 1999, ch. 662) by failing to prohibit respondents from *owning, possessing, purchasing, or receiving a firearm*. Three months later, on April 1, 2000, the Council published two (2) more mandatory restraining order forms that also violated Senate Bill 218 by failing to prohibit *owning or possessing* a firearm, bringing the total number of mandatory but void and unenforceable California Judicial Council restraining order forms published that year to thirteen (13).

There is no question this series of publishing mistakes occurred as set forth in this book. The public record shows that the forms DV-110, DV-130, and MC-220 were void and unenforceable throughout 1999, and that all of the state's restraining order forms were void throughout 2000. The public record also demonstrates that the Judicial Council failed to correctly revise the rest of California's restraining order forms to conform to statute for periods ranging from one (1) to seven (7) years after the forms were voided by the enactment of Senate Bill 218 by the California Legislature on January 1, 2000.

There is also no disputing that the Judicial Council failed to inform the public that most of the restraining order forms the Council published between 1999 and 2007 were void and unenforceable, or that, since no statutes of limitations apply to void orders, these orders continue to this day to be void and subject to direct and collateral attack at any time. Nor did the Judicial Council tell the public that thousands of presumably innocent African American respondents may have been falsely arrested and imprisoned without notice or a prior hearing as a direct and inevitable consequence of these void restraining order forms.

All the documents you need to understand this series of Judicial Council publishing mistakes are in your hand. This book is also your key to locating the source documents from which the illustrations came, and with those documents you can demand the Judicial Council take the necessary steps to acknowledge and remedy this series of publishing mistakes and their tragic consequences. These documents can also help to exonerate and compensate for their civil damages a whole generation of falsely imprisoned respondents.

Chapter 2
The Void Generation

Between 1999 and 2007 the governing arm of the state's Court system, the Judicial Council of California, published through its administrative agency, the Administrative Office of the Courts (AOC), a generation of restraining order forms that violated state and federal law. These unlawful forms voided the lives of a whole generation of presumably innocent African American and Hispanic respondents without a statutorily required warning notice or a prior hearing in open court, as the Constitutional guarantees of *due process* require.

On January 1, 1999, the Judicial Council published one revised and two new restraining order forms. The revised form was the criminal court restraining order form MC-220 (*Protective Order in Criminal Proceeding*). The two new forms were the domestic violence restraining form DV-110 (*Order to Show Cause and Temporary Restraining Order*) and the DV-130 (*Restraining Order After Hearing*) **[See Documents 1, 3 & 5]**.

1. The Void Firearm Restriction

When the DV-110 and DV-130 were first published on January 1, 1999, the Firearm Restriction notice printed in these two forms ordered respondents to give up any firearms they owned or possessed within 24 hours after issuance or 48 hours after service of the restraining order. But both deadlines came before the scheduled court hearing on the matter, which denied the respondents their Constitutional right to a prior court hearing before they could be deprived of any of their private property, so this flawed Firearm Restriction voided both forms as violations of *due process* **[See Documents 12 & 15]**:

FIREARM RESTRICTION
The restrained person is ordered to give up any firearm in or subject to his or her immediate possession or control within
a. 24 hours after issuance of this order
b. 48 hours after service of this order
c. other (*specify*):

At its October 27, 2000 general meeting the Judicial Council decided to revise the Firearm Restriction notice in the DV-110 and DV-130 to conform to federal law and the newly amended Family Code 6389(c) by including a reference to a prior noticed hearing **[See Documents 22 & 23]**. When these revised forms were published on January 1, 2001, their Firearm Restriction notices contained two new parenthetical phrases that referred to the presence or absence of the respondent at a prior court hearing (*If restrained* *person is present at hearing*) and (*If restrained person is not present at hearing*) **[See Documents 14 & 17]:**

FIREARM RESTRICTION

The restrained person is ordered to give up any firearm in or subject to his or her immediate possession or control within

a. 24 hours after issuance of this order (*If restrained person is present at hearing*)

b. 48 hours after service of this order (*If restrained person is not present at hearing*)

c. other (*specify*):

When the Judicial Council revised the MC-220 on January 1, 2001, the firearms relinquishment notice in this revised form failed to refer to the presence or absence of the respondent at a prior noticed hearing, voiding the form on publication. Nevertheless the Council repeatedly republished this void 2001 edition of the MC-220 twice a year for the next six (6) years, and the Courts continued to issue protective orders on this void form until it was eventually discontinued on January 1, 2007 **[See Document 19]:**

GOOD CAUSE APPEARING, THE COURT ORDERS that the above-named defendant

f. shall give up any firearm in or subject to his or her immediate possession or control within

(1) 24 hours after issuance of this order

(2) 48 hours after service of this order

(3) other (*specify*):

2. The Void Notice Regarding Firearms

When the DV-110, DV-130, and MC-220 were published on January 1, 1999 the Notice Regarding Firearms printed on the face of these forms informed respondents that at the noticed hearing on the matter the court had only the *authority* to order the relinquishment of firearms. The ambiguity of this notice denied respondents their due process right to a definite order, which made the forms *void for vagueness* **[See Documents 1, 3 & 5].**

Then on January 1, 2000 the newly enacted Senate Bill 218 amended Family Code Section 6389(f) and Penal Code Section 12021(g)(3) to order that the Judicial Council of California *shall provide notice on all protective orders that the respondent is prohibited from owning, possessing, purchasing, or receiving a firearm while the protective order is in effect* **[See Appendix E & Appendix F].**

But the Judicial Council violated Senate Bill 218 and amended Family Code Section 6389(f) and Penal Code Section 12021(g)(3) by failing to include a Notice Regarding Firearms prohibiting respondents from *owning, possessing, purchasing, or receiving a firearm* in any of the eleven (11) restraining order forms the Judicial Council published or republished on January 1, 2000 **[See Documents 1, 3, 5, 25, 27, 30, 38, 41, 42, 43 & 45]**. Nor did the Judicial Council include this warning notice in the two (2) additional restraining order forms the Council published on April 1, 2000 **[See Documents 32 & 35]**.

Where any of the prohibition notices in the remainder of California's restraining order forms referred to firearms at all, they prohibited only *purchasing or attempting to purchase, receiving or attempting to receive, or otherwise obtaining a firearm*:

NOTICE REGARDING FIREARMS

Any person subject to a restraining order is *prohibited from purchasing or attempting to purchase, receiving or attempting to receive, or otherwise obtaining a firearm.*

It was not until July 1, 2000, six (6) months after the Legislature's January 1, 2000 deadline, that the Judicial Council eventually revised the DV-110, DV-130, and MC-220 to conform to the requirements of Senate Bill 218 by including a Notice Regarding Firearms that prohibited respondents from *owning or possessing a firearm* **[See Documents 2, 4 & 6]**:

NOTICE REGARDING FIREARMS

Any person subject to a restraining order is prohibited from *owning, possessing, purchasing or attempting to purchase, receiving or attempting to receive, or otherwise obtaining a firearm.*

3. The Consequences

In an attempt to insure that no one would be prosecuted for violating the radically new firearms prohibitions imposed by Senate Bill 218 when they had never been told of the law's existence, the Legislature slipped an important qualifier into the second sentence of Penal Code Section 12021(g)(2) binding both the police and the Courts: *This subdivision does not apply unless a copy of the restraining order personally served on the person against whom the restraining order is issued contains a notice in bold print (1) stating that the person is prohibited from owning or possessing or attempting to own or possess a firearm and (2) specifying the penalties for violating this subdivision, or a court has provided actual verbal notice of the firearm prohibition and penalty as provided in Section 6304 of the Family Code* **[See Appendix F]**.

But the Judicial Council failed to inform the Courts that these restraining order forms did not contain the required warning notices until April 17, 2000, and to date the Judicial Council has never informed the press and the public that these restraining order forms were void **[See Documents 7 & 8]**. The Council also failed to revise any of these void restraining order forms to conform to the notice requirements of Senate Bill 218 and

Family Code Section 6389(f) and Penal Code Section 12021(g)3) for periods ranging from one (1) to more than seven (7) years after the state Legislature's January 1, 2000 deadline **[See Documents 14, 17, 19, 26, 29, 31, 34, 37, 39, 40, 41, 42, 44 & 46.**

As a consequence of these Judicial Council publishing mistakes, the California Courts were compelled to issue a whole generation of restraining orders on these mandatory but void and unenforceable forms. And since both the police and the Courts vigorously enforce most restraining orders, these void Judicial Council forms may have falsely imprisoned and voided the lives of a whole generation of presumably innocent respondents who were wrongfully snatched from California's oppressed minority communities and wrongfully incarcerated **[See Appendix C and Appendix D].**

Chapter 3
Senate Bill 218

On January 1, 2000 the California Legislature enacted Senate Bill 218, which amended among other statutes, Family Code Section 6389 and Penal Code Section 12021. These amendments

– Prohibited anyone from *owning, possessing, purchasing, or receiving a firearm* while they are the subject of a temporary or permanent restraining order.

– Ordered the Judicial Council to print a warning notice on all restraining order forms in bold type prohibiting respondents from *owning, possessing, purchasing, or receiving a firearm* while the protective order is in effect.

– Forbade the Courts from convicting respondents for allegedly violating Penal Code Section 12021(g)(2) unless the restraining order form personally served on the restrained person contained a notice in bold print specifically prohibiting the respondent from *owning or possessing or attempting to own or possess a firearm.*

1. Family Code Section 6389

Senate Bill 218 amended Family Code Section 6389 **[See Appendix E]**

– **Section 6389(a)** was amended to provide in pertinent part that *A person subject to a protective order...shall not own, possess, purchase, or receive a firearm while that protective order is in effect.*

– **Section 6389(b)** was amended to provide in pertinent part *The Judicial Council shall provide notice on all forms requesting a protective order that, at the hearing for a protective order, the respondent shall be ordered to relinquish possession or control of any firearms.*

– **Section 6389(c)** was amended to provide in pertinent part that *If the respondent is present in court at a duly noticed hearing, the court shall order the respondent to relinquish any firearm in that person's immediate possession or control, or subject to that person's immediate possession or control, within 24 hours of the order.... If the respondent is not present at the hearing, the respondent shall relinquish the firearm within 48 hours after being served with the order.*

– **Section 6389(f)** was amended to provide in pertinent part that *The restraining order requiring a person to relinquish a firearm pursuant to subdivision (c) shall state on its face that the respondent is prohibited from owning, possessing, purchasing, or receiving a firearm* while the protective order is in effect.

2. Penal Code Section 12021

Senate Bill 218 also amended Penal Code Section 12021 **[See Appendix F]**

– **Section 12021(g)(2)** was amended to provide in pertinent part that *Every person who owns or possesses a firearm knowing the he or she is prohibited from doing so by the provisions of a protective order...is guilty of a public offense.*

– **Section 12021(g)(2)** was also amended to provide in pertinent part that *This subdivision does not apply unless a copy of the restraining order personally served on the person against whom the restraining order is issued contains a notice in bold print stating...that the person is prohibited from owning or possessing or attempting to own or possess a firearm...or a court has provided actual verbal notice of the firearm prohibition.*

– **Section 12021(g)(3)** was amended to provide in pertinent part that the *Judicial Council shall provide notice on all protective orders that the respondent is prohibited from owning, possessing, purchasing, or receiving a firearm while the protective order is in effect.*

Chapter 4
The Judicial Council's Mistakes

California may have suffered from bigger and more serious bureaucratic blunders than the ones revealed in this book. We cannot know for certain, larger mistakes may await discovery. But few of the previous mistakes by the state's governing agencies that the public has so far been told about have approached the scale of these massive publishing mistakes by the Judicial Council of California.

This is a picture book of key pages copied from self-authenticating public documents which irrefutably demonstrate that between January 1, 1999 and January 1, 2007 the Judicial Council published a generation of void and unenforceable restraining order forms. These void forms compelled the California Courts to violate Constitutional due process guarantees and state and federal statutory law, and voided the lives of a whole generation of presumably innocent young African American and Hispanic respondents.

Here is how it happened:

1. The Judicial Council Forms

If someone stalks, threatens, or abuses another person, the targeted victim can ask a court to issue a restraining order to try to keep the abuser at bay. To issue a restraining order a judge must fill out and sign one of the many restraining order forms the Judicial Council of California publishes semi-annually for use by the Courts and the public.

The Judicial Council of California is the governing arm of the state's Court system, established by the California Constitution to set the direction for *improving the quality of justice and advancing its consistent, independent, impartial, and accessible administration for the benefit of the public.* Under the authority of Article 6, Section 6(d), of the California Constitution, the Judicial Council adopts rules for court practice and procedure that conform with governing law, and all judges are required to obey and cooperate with the Judicial Council's published rules and decisions.

The Judicial Council is also required by law to prescribe by rule the form and content of the official restraining order forms issued by the state Courts. California Government Code Section 68511 further provides that when any such form has been prescribed by the Council, no Court may use a different form which has as its aim the same functions as that for which the Council's prescribed form is designed.

Government Code Section 68511 also requires the Judicial Council to periodically report to the Legislature on any statutory changes needed to achieve uniformity in the official forms used by the Courts and the public. To achieve this objective, the Council's executive arm, the Administrative Office of the Courts (AOC), sends proposals for new or revised forms to all state Courts twice a year, usually in April and October, for their review and comments. If the Courts suggest that a new or revised form is needed, an Advisory Committee will place a recommendation to that effect on the Agenda for the Council's next general meeting.

The Council's Rules and Projects Committee will then review and pass on the Advisory Committee's recommendation, or may submit its own. The Judicial Council may then adopt, modify, or reject the proposed form, but if a particular restraining order form is adopted at a Council meeting, the state Courts are then required to issue all of their new restraining orders on the adopted form effective the following January 1 or July 1.

2. The Void Forms

These are important forms, upon which the very lives of endangered people may depend, so it is vitally important that any firearms prohibitions printed in the Judicial Council's mandatory forms must conform to the requirements of governing law. A restraining order issued on a Judicial Council form which fails to conform to the requirements of the law in effect at the time the Court issued the order is void and unenforceable, a legal nullity over which no Court anywhere has or can have the jurisdiction or authority to issue, uphold, or enforce at any time, against any person, or for any reason whatsoever **[See Appendix G]**.

Nor can anyone be arrested for violating a void restraining order. Such arrests violate the Constitutionally guaranteed right to due process. But that was the probable and foreseeable consequence of this generation of void orders for the thousands of presumably innocent respondents who may have been imprisoned for allegedly violating firearms restrictions and prohibitions that were in fact missing from many of the Judicial Council's published forms from January 1, 1999 until the last of this generation of void forms were finally dropped from the commercial forms books on January 1, 2007 **[See Appendix D]**.

3. The Void Restriction and Notice

On January 1, 1999 the Judicial Council of California published one revised and two new restraining order forms containing firearms prohibition notices that violated due process. The revised form was the criminal court restraining order Form MC-220 (*Protective Order in Criminal Proceeding*) (Rev. January 1, 1999). The two new forms were the domestic violence restraining order Forms DV-110 (*Order to Show Cause and Temporary Restraining Order*) (New Jan. 1, 1999) and DV-130 (*Restraining Order After Hearing*) (New January 1, 1999).

a. The Firearm Restriction

The Firearm Restriction in the January 1, 1999 editions of the DV-110 and DV-130 ordered respondents to relinquish their firearms before they had an opportunity appear in court to defend themselves at the noticed hearing. But this provision denied respondents their Constitutional right to a hearing in open court before they could be legally required to relinquish any private property, including their firearms, which voided both forms on publication as violations of due process **[See Documents 1 & 3].**

b. The Notice Regarding Firearms

While the Firearm Restriction notice in the January 1, 1999 editions of the DV-110 and DV-130 ordered respondents to immediately surrender their firearms, this notice was contradicted by the Notice Regarding Firearms printed in the Forms DV-110, DV-130, and MC-220, which informed respondents that it was only at the scheduled hearing on the matter that the Court *has authority* to order them to relinquish their firearms. The ambiguity of these contradictory notices denied respondents their Constitutional due process right to a definite order, making all three of these restraining order forms *void for vagueness* on publication **[See Documents 1, 3, 5, 12 & 15].**

c. The Mandate of Senate Bill 218

The Judicial Council republished the January 1, 1999 editions of the DV-110, DV-130, and MC-220 on January 1, 2000. But the newly enacted Senate Bill 218 now required that all restraining order forms must contain specific firearms prohibition notices, notices the Judicial Council neglected to include in any of these newly published and republished forms **[See Appendix E & Appendix F].**

Senate Bill 218 amended Family Code Section 6389(b) to order the Judicial Council to provide a notice on all forms requesting a protective order that, at the hearing on the protective order, the respondent *shall* be ordered to relinquish possession or control of any firearms. But the Judicial Council failed to revise the Notice Regarding Firearms in the DV-110, DV-130, and MC-220 to inform respondents the Court *will* order the relinquishment of firearms until July 1, 2000, six (6) months after the enactment of Senate Bill 218 **[See Documents 2, 4 & 6].**

Senate Bill 218 also amended Family Code Section 6389(f) and Penal Code Section 12021(g)(3) to order that the Judicial Council must provide a printed notice on all restraining order forms that respondents are prohibited from *owning, possessing, purchasing, or receiving a firearm*. But the Judicial Council failed to revise the Notice Regarding Firearms in the DV-110, DV-130, and MC-220 to prohibit *owning or possessing a firearm* until July 1, 2000, six (6) months after the January 1, 2000 deadline set by the Legislature in Senate Bill 218 **[See Documents 2, 4 & 6].**

Finally, Senate Bill 218 amended Family Code Section 6389(c) to require that if the respondent was *present* in court at a *duly noticed hearing*, they were ordered to relinquish possession or control of any firearms within 24 hours of the issuance of the order. If the respondent was *not present* at the hearing, they were required to relinquish any firearms within 48 hours of service of the order. But the Judicial Council failed to revise the Firearm Restriction in the DV-110 and DV-130 to refer to a prior court hearing until January 1, 2001, one (1) year after the enactment of S.B. 218 **[See Documents 14 & 17].**

When the Judicial Council revised the MC-220 on January 1, 2001, the Council failed to include a reference in the firearm restriction notice to the presence or absence of the respondent at a prior noticed hearing on the matter, which voided the form on publication. Nevertheless, the Council repeatedly republished this void January 1, 2001 revision of the MC-220 for the next six (6) years, and the criminal Courts continued to issue protective orders on this void form until the MC-220 was discontinued on January 1, 2007 **[See Document 19].**

5. The Other Void Forms

Senate Bill 218 amended Family Code Section 6389(f) and Penal Code Section 12021(g)(3) to require that as of January 1, 2000 *all* of the state's restraining order forms must contain a Notice Regarding Firearms prohibiting respondents from *owning, possessing, purchasing, or receiving a firearm.* But although the Judicial Council acknowledged in an April 17, 2000 Advisory Committee report that the required firearms prohibitions were missing from the DV-110, DV-130, and MC-220, it appears the Council failed to realize that these firearms prohibitions were also missing from ten (10) other restraining order forms for periods ranging from three (3) to more than seven (7) years after the enactment of Senate Bill 218 **[See Documents 7 & 8].**

a. Juvenile Violence Form JV-250

When the Judicial Council revised the Juvenile Violence Form JV-250 on January 1, 2000 the violations notice prohibited only *purchasing or attempting to purchase, receiving or attempting to receive a firearm* and the Firearm Restriction failed to refer to a prior noticed hearing. The Judicial Council failed to conform the JV-250 to statute with a warning notice prohibiting *owning, possessing, purchasing, or receiving a firearm* until January 1, 2003, three (3) years after the enactment of Senate Bill 218 **[See Documents 39 & 40].**

b. Civil Harassment Forms CH-120 and CH-140

When the Judicial Council republished the revised January 1, 1999 editions of the Civil Harassment Forms CH-120 and CH-140 on January 1, 2000, the warning notices prohibited only *purchasing or attempting to purchase, receiving or attempting to receive, or otherwise obtaining a firearm*. The Judicial Council failed to conform the CH-120 and CH-140 to statute with a warning notice prohibiting *owning, possessing, purchasing, or attempting to purchase, receiving or attempting to receive, or otherwise obtaining a firearm* until January 1, 2003, three (3) years after the enactment of Senate Bill 218 **[See Documents 27, 28, 29, 30 & 31]**.

c. Workplace Violence Forms WV-120 and WV-140

When the Judicial Council published the new Workplace Violence Forms WV-120 and WV-140 on January 1, 2000 the violations notices in the forms warned respondents that *Violation of this order is a misdemeanor*. The Judicial Council failed to conform the WV-120 and WV-140 to statute with violations notices prohibiting *owning, possessing, purchasing or attempting to purchase, receiving or attempting to receive, or otherwise obtaining a firearm* until January 1, 2003, three (3) years after the enactment of Senate Bill 218 **[See Documents 43, 44, 45 & 46]**.

d. Emergency Protective Order Form 1295.90

When the Judicial Council revised the Emergency Protective Order Form 1295.90 on January 1, 2000 the violations notices prohibited *purchasing or attempting to purchase or otherwise obtaining a firearm*. The Judicial Council failed to conform the 1295.90 to statute with violations notices prohibiting *owning, possessing, purchasing, receiving, or attempting to purchase or receive a firearm* until January 1, 2004, four (4) years after the enactment of Senate Bill 218 **[See Documents 25 & 26]**.

e. Elder Abuse Forms EA-120 and EA-130

When the Judicial Council published the new Elder Abuse restraining order Forms EA-120 and EA-130 on April 1, 2000 the violations notice in the EA-120 warned respondents that *Violation of this order may be punishable as contempt of court,* and the violations notice in the EA-130 prohibited only *obtaining or attempting to obtain or purchase a firearm*. The Judicial Council failed to conform the EA-120 and EA-130 to statute with a violations notice prohibiting *owning, possessing, purchasing, or receiving, or attempting to purchase or receive a firearm* until July 1, 2004, four and a half (4.5) years after the enactment of Senate Bill 218 **[See Documents 32, 33, 34, 35, 36 & 37]**.

f. Transitional Housing Forms TH-110 and TH-130

Finally, when the Judicial Council republished the Transitional Housing restraining order Forms TH-110 and TH-130 the violations notices warned respondents that *Violation of this order is a misdemeanor*. The public record demonstrates that as of January 1, 2007, seven (7) years after the enactment of Senate Bill 218, the Judicial Council had not yet conformed the TH-110 and TH-130 to statute with a violations notice warning respondents they are prohibited form *owning or possessing a firearm*. Nevertheless, the Council repeatedly republished these void July 1, 1992 editions of the TH-110 and TH-130, and the Courts continued to issue restraining orders on these void forms, for at least the seven (7) years prior to January 1, 2007.**[See Documents 41 & 42].**

6. The First Report

On April 17, 2000, three months after the enactment of Senate Bill 218, the Judicial Council's Center for Families, Children and the Courts notified the Courts in a report personally initialed by the Director of the Center that the firearms prohibition notices in the January 1, 1999 editions of the DV-110, DV-130, and MC-220 violated the new Senate Bill 218. In a report titled Technical Revisions to Domestic Violence Forms the Center noted that the California Legislature had amended Penal Code Section 12021(g)(2), effective January 1, 2000, to prohibit restraining order respondents from *owning, possessing, purchasing, or receiving a firearm* **[See Document 7].**

The report also noted that amended Penal Code Section 12021(g)(3) ordered the Judicial Council to print a warning notice on the face of all protective orders prohibiting respondents from *owning, possessing, purchasing, or receiving a firearm*. Significantly, this report also told the Courts that criminal penalties for allegedly violating Penal Code Section 12021(g)(2) did not apply unless the restraining order form personally served on the restrained person contained a warning notice prohibiting the respondent from *owning or possessing or attempting to own or possess a firearm* **[See Documents 7 & 8].**

In this report the Judicial Council also confessed to the Courts, in a paragraph titled Alternative Actions Considered, that in response to the requirements of Penal Code Section 12021(g)(3) the Council *considered creating a one-page form that could be attached to the appropriate forms,* but decided against publishing this Constitutionally and statutorily required warning notice because *attaching the warning to every restraining order might be burdensome to court clerks and individuals* **[See Document 8].**

7. The First Decision

On April 28, 2000, the Judicial Council met to consider, among other things, staff recommendations the Council revise the Notice Regarding Firearms in the restraining order forms DV-110, DV-130, and MC-220 to conform to the notice requirements of amended Penal Code Section 12021(g)(3). In response, the Council voted unanimously to revise the three forms, *effective July 1, 2000,* to include a Notice Regarding Firearms prohibiting respondents from *owning, possessing, purchasing, or receiving a firearm*. This binding Judicial Council decision confirmed that the previous January 1, 1999 editions of the DV-110, DV-130, and MC-220 were void as of the January 1, 2000 enactment of Senate Bill 218 **[See Documents 9, 10 & 11].**

8. The Second Report

On October 5, 2000 the Judicial Council's Family and Juvenile Law Advisory Committee sent a second report to the Courts informing them that the Firearm Restriction notice in the July 1, 2000 editions of the restraining order forms DV-110 and DV-130 ordered respondents to relinquish their firearms before they had an opportunity to appear and be heard at a noticed hearing. The report also noted that this Firearm Restriction notice violated the notice requirements of the newly enacted Senate Bill 218 and amended Family Code Section 6389(c) **[See Documents 20 & 21].**

9. The Second Decision

On October 27, 2000 the Judicial Council met to consider, among other things, staff recommendations that the Judicial Council was required to revise the Firearm Restriction in the restraining order forms DV-110 and DV-130 to conform to the notice requirements of Senate Bill 218 and amended Family Code Section 6389(c). In response to these recommendations, the Judicial Council voted unanimously to revise both forms, *effective January 1, 2001,* to *conform to recent statutory changes regarding firearm relinquishment* by including a Firearm Restriction notice referring to a prior noticed hearing. This binding Judicial Council decision confirmed that the previous July 1, 2000 editions of the DV-110 and DV-130 were void **[See Documents 22 & 24].**

10. Who Was Affected

Three years after the enactment of Senate Bill 218, three researchers from the UCLA School of Public Health conducted a statistical study of the active restraining orders listed in California's Domestic Violence Restraining Order System. The study concluded that as of June 6, 2003 there were *227,941* active restraining orders in the statewide database against adults, and that the majority of these restraining orders affected young men of color.

In 72.2% of the restraining orders listed in California's restraining order database a woman was to be protected and a man was to be restrained, and there were few mutual restraining orders. In 19.3% of the listed orders, the restrained person and the protected person were of the same sex. The numerical rates of these restraining orders (i.e., the number of restrained persons) were highest for *men* (1,496.6 per 100,000), *25-34 year olds* (1,366.8 per 100,000), and *persons of color* (2,437.5 per 100,000) **[See Appendix C].**

11. The Numbers Affected

In July of 2002, two and a half years after the enactment of Senate Bill 218, the California Department of Justice (DOJ) issued a report titled *Special Report to the Legislature on Senate Bill 1608 Arrests and court dispositions of felons and others arrested for firearms possession in California's 58 counties* prepared by the DOJ's Criminal Justice Statistics Center. The report analyzed and summarized the available statistical data on the number of people arrested statewide and by county in 1998, 1999, and 2000 for allegedly violating the prohibitions in Penal Code Sections 12021 or 12021.1 by *owning or possessing a firearm.*

This comprehensive DOJ study found that in 1999, when the forms DV-110, DV-130, and MC-220 were Constitutionally void, a total of *5,919* people were arrested for allegedly violating Penal Code Sections 12021 or 12021.1. According to this report, another *6,219* people were also arrested and jailed in the year 2000 for allegedly violating the same two Penal Code sections, after every restraining order form published by the Judicial Council was voided by the enactment of Senate Bill 218 on January 1, 2000. **[See Appendix D].**

12. California's Void Forms

Below is an alpha-numeric list of the thirteen (13) void forms referred to in this book and the years these restraining order forms were void **[See Appendix A & Appendix B].**

1. Civil Harassment Form CH-120 (*Order to Show Cause and Temporary Restraining Order*) – void three (3) years, January 1, 2000–January 1, 2003 **[See Documents 27, 28 & 29].**

2. Civil Harassment Form CH-140 (*Order After Hearing*) – void three (3) years, January 1, 2000–January 1, 2003 **[See Documents 30 & 31].**

3. Domestic Violence Form DV-110 (*Order to Show Cause and Temporary Restraining Order*) – void two (2) years, January 1, 1999–January 1, 2001 **[See Documents 1, 2, 12, 13 & 14].**

4. Domestic Violence Form DV-130 (*Restraining Order After Hearing*) – void two (2) years, January 1, 1999–January 1, 2001 **[See Documents 15, 16 & 17].**

5. Elder Abuse Form EA-120 (*Order to Show Cause and Temporary Restraining Order*) – void four and a quarter (4.25) years, April 1, 2000–July 1, 2004 **[See Documents 32, 33 & 34].**

6. Elder Abuse Form EA-130 (*Restraining Order After Hearing*) – void four and a quarter (4.25) years, April 1, 2000–July 1, 2004 **[See Documents 35, 36 & 37].**

7. Emergency Protective Order Form 1295.90/EPO-001 (*Emergency Protective Order*) – void four (4) years, January 1, 2000–January 1, 2004 **[See Documents 25 & 26]**.

8. Juvenile Violence Form JV-250 (*Restraining Order-Juvenile*) – void three (3) years, January 1, 2000–January 1, 2003 **[See Documents 38, 39 & 40]**.

9. Criminal Court Form MC-220 (*Protective Order In Criminal Proceeding*) – void eight (8) years, January 1, 1999–January 1, 2007 **[See Documents 5, 6, 18 & 19]**.

10. Transitional Housing Form TH-110 (*Order to Show Cause and Temporary Restraining Order*) – void at least seven (7) years, January 1, 2000–January 1, 2007+ **[See Document 41]**.

11. Transitional Housing Form TH-130 (*Order After Hearing*) – void at least seven (7) years, January 1, 2000–January 1, 2007+ **[See Document 42]**.

12. Workplace Violence Form WV-120 (*Order to Show Cause and Temporary Restraining Order*) – void three (3) years, January 1, 2000–January 1, 2003 **[See Documents 43 & 44]**.

13. Workplace Violence Form WV-140 (*Order After Hearing On Petition Of Employer For Injunction Prohibiting Violence Or Threats Of Violence Against Employee*) – void three (3) years, January 1, 2000–January 1, 2003 **[See Documents 45 & 46]**.

Chapter 5
The Void Notice

Document 1

Form DV-110 (New Jan. 1, 1999) p. 4

The Judicial Council published the domestic violence temporary restraining order Form DV-110 (*Order to Show Cause and Temporary Restraining Order*) on January 1, 1999, one (1) year before the California Legislature enacted Senate Bill 218, Penal Code Section 12021(g)(3), and Family Code Sections 6389(b) and 6389(f) on January 1, 2000.

The Notice Regarding Firearms on page 4 of this new form conformed to the notice requirements Penal Code Section 12021(g) by prohibiting respondents from *purchasing or attempting to purchase, receiving or attempting to receive, or otherwise obtaining a firearm.* However, the Notice Regarding Firearms also violated the due process right to a definite order by ambiguously warning respondents that at the hearing on the matter the Court had only the *authority* to order firearms relinquished.

When Judicial Council republished this January 1, 1999 edition of the DV-110 on January 1, 2000, the Notice Regarding Firearms violated the notice requirements of the newly amended Family Code Section 6389(f) and Penal Code Section 12021(g)(3) by failing to prohibit respondents from *owning, possessing, purchasing, or receiving a firearm.* The Notice Regarding Firearms also violated the notice requirements of the newly amended Family Code Section 6389(b) by failing to warn respondents that at the hearing on the matter the Court *shall* order firearms relinquished.

Extract from Document 1

NOTICE REGARDING FIREARMS

Any person subject to a restraining order is prohibited from *purchasing or attempting to purchase, receiving or attempting to receive, or otherwise obtaining* a firearm. Such conduct is subject to a $1,000 fine and imprisonment. At the hearing on this matter, the court has *authority* to order that the person subject to these orders relinquish any firearms and not own or possess any firearms during the period of the restraining order. If restraining orders are issued, the restrained person may not be able to possess a firearm.

PERSON SEEKING ORDER (name):	CASE NUMBER:
PERSON TO BE RESTRAINED (name):	

WHAT FORMS YOU SHOULD FILE IN RESPONSE AND WHEN TO FILE THEM

You do not have to pay any fee to file responsive declarations in response to this *Order to Show Cause* (including a completed *Income and Expense Declaration* or *Financial Statement (Simplified)* that will show your finances). The original of the *Responsive Declaration* must be filed with the court and a copy served on the other party at least five court days before the hearing date (unless the judge has shortened time, see item 12 above in this *Order to Show Cause and Temporary Restraining Order*).

NOTICE REGARDING CHILD SUPPORT

If you have children from this relationship, the court is required to order payment of child support based on the income of both parents. The amount of child support may be large and normally continues until the child is 18. You should supply the court with information about your finances. Otherwise the child support order will be made without your input.

NOTICE REGARDING ENFORCEMENT OF THIS ORDER

This order is effective when made. It is enforceable anywhere in California by any law enforcement agency that has received the order, is shown a copy of the order, or has verified its existence on the California Law Enforcement Telecommunications System (CLETS). If proof of service on the restrained person has not been received, and the restrained person was not present at the court hearing, the law enforcement agency shall advise the restrained person of the terms of the order and then shall enforce it.

Violation of this restraining order may be punished as a contempt of court, a misdemeanor, punishable by one year in jail or a $1000 fine, or both, or a felony. Taking or concealing a child in violation of this order may be a felony and punishable by confinement in state prison, a fine, or both.

This order is enforceable in all 50 states, the District of Columbia, all tribal lands, and all U.S. territories and shall be enforced as if it were an order of that jurisdiction. Violations of this order are subject to state and federal criminal penalties.

If you travel across state or tribal boundaries with the intent to violate the order (including committing a crime of violence causing bodily injury), you may be convicted of a federal offense under VAWA (section 2261(a)(1)). You may also be convicted of a federal offense if you cause the protected person to cross a state or tribal boundary for this purpose (section 2262(a)(2)).

NOTICE REGARDING FIREARMS

Any person subject to a restraining order is prohibited from purchasing or attempting to purchase, receiving or attempting to receive, or otherwise obtaining a firearm. Such conduct is subject to a $1,000 fine and imprisonment. At the hearing on this matter, the court has authority to order that the person subject to these orders relinquish any firearms and not own or possess any firearms during the period of the restraining order. If restraining orders are issued, the restrained person may not be able to possess a firearm. Under federal law, the issuance of a restraining order after hearing will generally prohibit the restrained person from owning, accepting, transporting, or possessing firearms or ammunition. A violation of this prohibition is a separate federal crime.

CLERK'S CERTIFICATE

[SEAL]

I certify that the foregoing *Order to Show Cause and Temporary Restraining Order (CLETS)* is a true and correct copy of the original on file in the court.

Date: _____   Clerk, by _____ , Deputy

DV-110 [New January 1, 1999]   **ORDER TO SHOW CAUSE AND TEMPORARY RESTRAINING ORDER**
(CLETS) (Domestic Violence Prevention)   Page four of four

21

Document 2

Form DV-110 (Rev. July 1, 2000) p. 4

The Judicial Council revised the domestic violence temporary restraining order DV-110 (*Order to Show Cause and Temporary Restraining Order*) on July 1, 2000, six (6) months after the California Legislature enacted Senate Bill 218, Penal Code Section 12021(g)(3), and Family Code Section 6389(f) on January 1, 2000.

The Notice Regarding Firearms on page 4 of this revision conformed to the notice requirements of the newly amended Family Code Section 6389(f) and Penal Code Section 12021(g)(3) by prohibiting respondents from *owning, possessing, purchasing or attempting to purchase, receiving or attempting to receive, or otherwise obtaining a firearm*. The Notice Regarding Firearms also conformed to the notice requirements of the newly amended Family Code 6389(b) by warning respondents that at the hearing on the matter the Court *will* order firearms relinquished.

Extract from Document 2

NOTICE REGARDING FIREARMS

Any person subject to a restraining order is prohibited from *owning, possessing, purchasing or attempting to purchase, receiving or attempting to receive, or otherwise obtaining a firearm*. Such conduct is subject to a $1,000 fine and imprisonment. At the hearing on this matter, the court *will* order that the person subject to these orders shall relinquish any firearms and not own or possess any firearms during the period of the restraining order. If restraining orders are issued, the restrained person may not be able to possess a firearm.

PERSON SEEKING ORDER *(name):*	CASE NUMBER:
PERSON TO BE RESTRAINED *(name):*	

WHAT FORMS YOU SHOULD FILE IN RESPONSE AND WHEN TO FILE THEM

You do not have to pay any fee to file responsive declarations in response to this *Order to Show Cause* (including a completed *Income and Expense Declaration* or *Financial Statement (Simplified)* that will show your finances). The original of the *Responsive Declaration* must be filed with the court and a copy served on the other party at least five court days before the hearing date (unless the judge has shortened time; see item 12 above in this *Order to Show Cause and Temporary Restraining Order).*

NOTICE REGARDING CHILD SUPPORT

If you have children from this relationship, the court is required to order payment of child support based on the income of both parents. The amount of child support may be large and normally continues until the child is 18. You should supply the court with information about your finances. Otherwise the child support order will be made without your input.

NOTICE REGARDING ENFORCEMENT OF THIS ORDER

This order is effective when made. It is enforceable anywhere in California by any law enforcement agency that has received the order, is shown a copy of the order, or has verified its existence on the California Law Enforcement Telecommunications System (CLETS). If proof of service on the restrained person has not been received, and the restrained person was not present at the court hearing, the law enforcement agency shall advise the restrained person of the terms of the order and then shall enforce it.

Violation of this restraining order may be punished as a contempt of court; a misdemeanor, punishable by one year in jail, a $1,000 fine, or both; or a felony. Taking or concealing a child in violation of this order may be a felony and punishable by confinement in state prison, a fine, or both.

This order is enforceable in all 50 states, the District of Columbia, all tribal lands, and all U.S. territories and shall be enforced as if it were an order of that jurisdiction. Violations of this order are subject to state and federal criminal penalties.

If you travel across state or tribal boundaries with the intent to violate the order (including committing a crime of violence causing bodily injury), you may be convicted of a federal offense under VAWA (section 2261(a)(1)). You may also be convicted of a federal offense if you cause the protected person to cross a state or tribal boundary for this purpose (section 2262(a)(2)).

NOTICE REGARDING FIREARMS

Any person subject to a restraining order is prohibited from owning, possessing, purchasing or attempting to purchase, receiving or attempting to receive, or otherwise obtaining a firearm. Such conduct is subject to a $1,000 fine and imprisonment. At the hearing on this matter, the court will order that the person subject to these orders shall relinquish any firearms and not own or possess any firearms during the period of the restraining order. If restraining orders are issued, the restrained person may not possess a firearm. Under federal law, the issuance of a restraining order after hearing will generally prohibit the restrained person from owning, accepting, transporting, or possessing firearms or ammunition. A violation of this prohibition is a separate federal crime.

CLERK'S CERTIFICATE

[SEAL]

I certify that the foregoing *Order to Show Cause and Temporary Restraining Order (CLETS)* is a true and correct copy of the original on file in the court.

Date: _____   Clerk, by _____ , Deputy

ORDER TO SHOW CAUSE AND TEMPORARY RESTRAINING ORDER
(CLETS) (Domestic Violence Prevention)

Document 3

Form DV-130 (New Jan. 1, 1999) p. 3

The Judicial Council published the domestic violence post-hearing restraining order form DV-130 (*Restraining Order After Hearing*) on January 1, 1999, one (1) year before the California Legislature enacted Senate Bill 218, Penal Code Section 12021(g)(3), and Family Code Section 6389(f) on January 1, 2000.

The Notice Regarding Firearms on page 3 of this new form conformed to the notice requirements Penal Code Section 12021(g) by prohibiting respondents from *purchasing or attempting to purchase, receiving or attempting to receive, or otherwise obtaining a firearm.*

However, when the Judicial Council republished this January 1, 1999 edition of the DV-130 on January 1, 2000, the Notice Regarding Firearms violated the notice requirements of the newly amended Family Code Section 6389(f) and Penal Code Section 12021(g)(3) by failing to prohibit respondents from *owning, possessing, purchasing, or receiving a firearm.*

Extract from Document 3

NOTICE REGARDING FIREARMS

Any person subject to a restraining order is prohibited from *purchasing or attempting to purchase, receiving or attempting to receive, or otherwise obtaining a firearm.* Such conduct is subject to a $1,000 fine and imprisonment.

PROTECTED PERSON (name):	CASE NUMBER:
RESTRAINED PERSON (name):	

12. ☐ A copy of this order shall be given to the additional law enforcement agencies listed below by the protected person or the protected person's attorney:

Law enforcement agency   Address

13. Any attachments noted in items 5, 6, and 7 of this order are attached hereto, incorporated herein, and made a part of this order. Number of pages attached: _____

Date:

_____
JUDICIAL OFFICER

This order is effective when made. It is enforceable anywhere in all 50 states, the District of Columbia, all tribal lands, and all U.S. territories and shall be enforced as if it were an order of that jurisdiction by any law enforcement agency that has received the order, is shown a copy of the order, or has verified its existence on the California Law Enforcement Telecommunications System (CLETS). If proof of service on the restrained person has not been received, and the restrained person was not present at the court hearing, the law enforcement agency shall advise the restrained person of the terms of the order and then shall enforce it. Violations of this restraining order are subject to state and federal criminal penalties. This order meets all Full Faith and Credit requirements of the Violence Against Women Act, 18 U.S.C. 2265 (1994) (VAWA). This court has jurisdiction of the parties and the subject matter; the defendant has been afforded notice and a timely opportunity to be heard as provided by the laws of this jurisdiction. This order is valid and entitled to enforcement in this and all other jurisdictions.

NOTICE REGARDING FIREARMS

Any person subject to a restraining order is prohibited from purchasing or attempting to purchase, receiving or attempting to receive, or otherwise obtaining a firearm. Such conduct is subject to a $1,000 fine and imprisonment. Under federal law, the issuance of a restraining order after hearing will generally prohibit the restrained person from owning, accepting, transporting, or possessing firearms or ammunition. A violation of this prohibition is a separate federal crime.

CLERK'S CERTIFICATE

[SEAL]

I certify that the foregoing *Restraining Order After Hearing (CLETS)* is a true and correct copy of the original on file in the court.

Date: _____   Clerk, by _____ , Deputy

DV-130 [New January 1, 1999]   **RESTRAINING ORDER AFTER HEARING (CLETS)**   Page three of three
                                     (Domestic Violence Prevention)

25

Document 4

Form DV-130 (Rev. July 1, 2000) p. 3

The Judicial Council revised the domestic violence post-hearing restraining order Form DV-130 (*Restraining Order After Hearing*) on July 1, 2000, six (6) months after the California Legislature enacted Senate Bill 218, Penal Code Section 12021(g)(3), and Family Code Section 6389(f) on January 1, 2000.

The Notice Regarding Firearms on page 3 of this revision conformed to the notice requirements of the newly amended Family Code Section 6389(f) and Penal Code Section 12021(g)(3) by prohibiting respondents from *owning, possessing, purchasing or attempting to purchase, receiving or attempting to receive, or otherwise obtaining a firearm.*

Extract from Document 4

NOTICE REGARDING FIREARMS

Any person subject to a restraining order is prohibited from *owning, possessing, purchasing or attempting to purchase, receiving or attempting to receive, or otherwise obtaining a firearm.* Such conduct is subject to a $1,000 fine and imprisonment.

PROTECTED PERSON *(name)*:	CASE NUMBER:
RESTRAINED PERSON *(name)*:	

12. ☐ A copy of this order shall be given to the additional law enforcement agencies listed below by the protected person or the protected person's attorney:

<u>Law enforcement agency</u>   <u>Address</u>

13. Any attachments noted in items 5, 6, and 7 of this order are attached hereto, incorporated herein, and made a part of this order. Number of pages attached: _____

Date:

_____
JUDICIAL OFFICER

This order is effective when made. It is enforceable anywhere in all 50 states, the District of Columbia, all tribal lands, and all U.S. territories and shall be enforced as if it were an order of that jurisdiction by any law enforcement agency that has received the order, is shown a copy of the order, or has verified its existence on the California Law Enforcement Telecommunications System (CLETS). If proof of service on the restrained person has not been received, and the restrained person was not present at the court hearing, the law enforcement agency shall advise the restrained person of the terms of the order and then shall enforce it. Violations of this restraining order are subject to state and federal criminal penalties. This order meets all Full Faith and Credit requirements of the Violence Against Women Act, 18 U.S.C. 2265 (1994) (VAWA). This court has jurisdiction of the parties and the subject matter; the defendant has been afforded notice and a timely opportunity to be heard as provided by the laws of this jurisdiction. This order is valid and entitled to enforcement in this and all other jurisdictions.

NOTICE REGARDING FIREARMS

Any person subject to a restraining order is prohibited from owning, possessing, purchasing or attempting to purchase, receiving or attempting to receive, or otherwise obtaining a firearm. Such conduct is subject to a $1,000 fine and imprisonment. Under federal law, the issuance of a restraining order after hearing will generally prohibit the restrained person from owning, accepting, transporting, or possessing firearms or ammunition. A violation of this prohibition is a separate federal crime.

CLERK'S CERTIFICATE

[SEAL]

I certify that the foregoing *Restraining Order After Hearing (CLETS)* is a true and correct copy of the original on file in the court.

Date: _____   Clerk, by _____ , Deputy

DV-130 [Rev. July 1, 2000]   **RESTRAINING ORDER AFTER HEARING (CLETS)**   **Page three of three**
(Domestic Violence Prevention)

27

Document 5

Form MC-220 (Rev. Jan. 1, 1999) p. 2

The Judicial Council revised the criminal court restraining order Form MC-220 (*Protective Order In Criminal Proceeding*) on January 1, 1999, one (1) year before the California Legislature enacted Senate Bill 218, Penal Code Section 12021(g)(3), and Family Code Sections 6389(b) and 6389(f) on January 1, 2000.

The Notice Regarding Firearms on page 2 of this revision conformed to the notice requirements of Penal Code Section 12021(g) by prohibiting respondents from *purchasing or attempting to purchase, receiving or attempting to receive, or otherwise obtaining a firearm*. However, this Notice Regarding Firearms also violated the due process right to a definite order by ambiguously warning respondents that at the hearing on the matter the Court had only the *authority* to order the relinquishment of firearms.

When the Judicial Council republished this January 1, 1999 revision of the MC-220 on January 1, 2000, the Notice Regarding Firearms violated the notice requirements of amended Family Code Section 6389(f) and Penal Code Section 12021(g)(3) by failing to prohibit respondents from *owning, possessing, purchasing, or receiving a firearm*. This Notice Regarding Firearms also violated the notice requirements of amended Family Code Section 6389(b) by failing to warn respondents that at the hearing on the matter the Court *shall* order the relinquishment of firearms.

Extract from Document 5

NOTICE REGARDING FIREARMS

Any person subject to a restraining order is prohibited from *purchasing or attempting to purchase, receiving or attempting to receive, or otherwise obtaining a firearm*. Such conduct is subject to a $1,000 fine and imprisonment. At the hearing on this matter, the court has *authority* to order that the person subject to these orders relinquish any firearms and not own or possess any firearms during the period of the restraining order. If restraining orders are issued, the restrained person may not be able to possess a firearm.

PEOPLE OF THE STATE OF CALIFORNIA vs.	CASE NUMBER:
DEFENDANT:	

CERTIFICATE OF COMPLIANCE WITH VAWA This ex parte/temporary protective order meets all Full Faith and Credit requirements of the Violence Against Women Act, 18 U.S.C. 2265 (1994) (VAWA). This court has jurisdiction over the parties and the subject matter; the restrained person has been afforded notice and a timely opportunity to be heard as provided by the laws of this jurisdiction. This order is valid and entitled to enforcement in this and all other jurisdictions.

NOTICE REGARDING NON-APPEARANCE AT HEARING

IF YOU HAVE BEEN PERSONALLY SERVED WITH A TEMPORARY RESTRAINING ORDER AND NOTICE OF HEARING, BUT YOU DO NOT APPEAR AT THE HEARING EITHER IN PERSON OR BY COUNSEL, AND A RESTRAINING ORDER IS ISSUED AT THE HEARING WHICH DOES NOT DIFFER FROM THE PRIOR TEMPORARY RESTRAINING ORDER, A COPY OF THE ORDER WILL BE SERVED UPON YOU BY MAIL AT THE FOLLOWING ADDRESS:

IF THAT ADDRESS IS NOT CORRECT OR YOU WISH TO VERIFY THAT THE TEMPORARY ORDER WAS MADE PERMANENT WITHOUT SUBSTANTIVE CHANGE, CONTACT THE CLERK OF THE COURT.

NOTICE REGARDING ENFORCEMENT OF THIS ORDER

This order is effective when made. It is enforceable anywhere in California by any law enforcement agency that has received the order, is shown a copy of the order, or has verified its existence on the California Law Enforcement Telecommunications System (CLETS). If proof of service on the restrained person has not been received, and the restrained person was not present at the court hearing, the law enforcement agency shall advise the restrained person of the terms of the order and then shall enforce it.

Violation of this restraining order may be punished as a contempt of court, a misdemeanor, punishable by one year in jail or a $1000 fine, or both, or a felony. Taking or concealing a child in violation of this order may be a felony and punishable by confinement in state prison, a fine, or both.

This order is enforceable in all 50 states, the District of Columbia, all tribal lands, and all U.S. territories and shall be enforced as if it were an order of that jurisdiction. Violations of this order are subject to state and federal criminal penalties.

If you travel across state or tribal boundaries with the intent to violate the order (including committing a crime of violence causing bodily injury), you may be convicted of a federal offense under VAWA (section 2261(a)(1)). You may also be convicted of a federal offense if you cause the protected person to cross a state or tribal boundary for this purpose (section 2262(a)(2)).

NOTICE REGARDING FIREARMS

Any person subject to a restraining order is prohibited from purchasing or attempting to purchase, receiving or attempting to receive, or otherwise obtaining a firearm. Such conduct is subject to a $1,000 fine and imprisonment. At the hearing on this matter, the court has authority to order that the person subject to these orders relinquish any firearms and not own or possess any firearms during the period of the restraining order. If restraining orders are issued, the restrained person may not be able to possess a firearm. Under federal law, the issuance of a restraining order after hearing will generally prohibit the restrained person from owning, accepting, transporting, or possessing firearms or ammunition. A violation of this prohibition is a separate federal crime.

Document 6

Form MC-220 (Rev. July 1, 2000) p. 2

The Judicial Council revised the criminal court restraining order Form MC-220 (*Protective Order In Criminal Proceeding*) on July 1, 2000, six (6) months after the California Legislature enacted Senate Bill 218, Penal Code Section 12021(g)(3), and Family Code Sections 6389(b) and 6389(f) on January 1, 2000.

The Notice Regarding Firearms on page 2 of this revision conformed to the notice requirements of amended Family Code Section 6389(f) and Penal Code Section 12021(g)(3) by prohibiting respondents from *owning, possessing, purchasing or attempting to purchase, receiving or attempting to receive, or otherwise obtaining a firearm*. The Notice Regarding Firearms also conformed to the notice requirements of Family Code Section 6389(b) by warning respondents that at the hearing on the matter the Court *will* order firearms relinquished.

Extract from Document 6

NOTICE REGARDING FIREARMS

Any person subject to a restraining order is prohibited from *owning, possessing, purchasing or attempting to purchase, receiving or attempting to receive, or otherwise obtaining a firearm*. Such conduct is subject to a $1,000 fine and imprisonment. At the hearing on this matter, the court *will* order that the person subject to these orders shall relinquish any firearms and not own or possess any firearms during the period of the restraining order. If restraining orders are issued, the restrained person may not possess a firearm.

PEOPLE OF THE STATE OF CALIFORNIA vs.	CASE NUMBER:
DEFENDANT:	

CERTIFICATE OF COMPLIANCE WITH VAWA This ex parte/temporary protective order meets all Full Faith and Credit requirements of the Violence Against Women Act, 18 U.S.C. 2265 (1994) (VAWA). This court has jurisdiction over the parties and the subject matter; the restrained person has been afforded notice and a timely opportunity to be heard as provided by the laws of this jurisdiction. This order is valid and entitled to enforcement in this and all other jurisdictions.

NOTICE REGARDING NON-APPEARANCE AT HEARING

IF YOU HAVE BEEN PERSONALLY SERVED WITH A TEMPORARY RESTRAINING ORDER AND NOTICE OF HEARING, BUT YOU DO NOT APPEAR AT THE HEARING EITHER IN PERSON OR BY COUNSEL, AND A RESTRAINING ORDER IS ISSUED AT THE HEARING WHICH DOES NOT DIFFER FROM THE PRIOR TEMPORARY RESTRAINING ORDER, A COPY OF THE ORDER WILL BE SERVED UPON YOU BY MAIL AT THE FOLLOWING ADDRESS:

IF THAT ADDRESS IS NOT CORRECT OR YOU WISH TO VERIFY THAT THE TEMPORARY ORDER WAS MADE PERMANENT WITHOUT SUBSTANTIVE CHANGE, CONTACT THE CLERK OF THE COURT.

NOTICE REGARDING ENFORCEMENT OF THIS ORDER

This order is effective when made. It is enforceable anywhere in California by any law enforcement agency that has received the order, is shown a copy of the order, or has verified its existence on the California Law Enforcement Telecommunications System (CLETS). If proof of service on the restrained person has not been received, and the restrained person was not present at the court hearing, the law enforcement agency shall advise the restrained person of the terms of the order and then shall enforce it.

Violation of this restraining order may be punished as a contempt of court; a misdemeanor, punishable by one year in jail, a $1,000 fine, or both; or a felony. Taking or concealing a child in violation of this order may be a felony and punishable by confinement in state prison, a fine, or both.

This order is enforceable in all 50 states, the District of Columbia, all tribal lands, and all U.S. territories and shall be enforced as if it were an order of that jurisdiction. Violations of this order are subject to state and federal criminal penalties.

If you travel across state or tribal boundaries with the intent to violate the order (including committing a crime of violence causing bodily injury), you may be convicted of a federal offense under VAWA (section 2261(a)(1)). You may also be convicted of a federal offense if you cause the protected person to cross a state or tribal boundary for this purpose (section 2262(a)(2)).

NOTICE REGARDING FIREARMS

Any person subject to a restraining order is prohibited from owning, possessing, purchasing or attempting to purchase, receiving or attempting to receive, or otherwise obtaining a firearm. Such conduct is subject to a $1,000 fine and imprisonment. At the hearing on this matter, the court will order that the person subject to these orders shall relinquish any firearms and not own or possess any firearms during the period of the restraining order. If restraining orders are issued, the restrained person may not possess a firearm. Under federal law, the issuance of a restraining order after hearing will generally prohibit the restrained person from owning, accepting, transporting, or possessing firearms or ammunition. A violation of this prohibition is a separate federal crime.

MC-220 [Rev. July 1, 2000] **PROTECTIVE ORDER IN CRIMINAL PROCEEDING (CLETS)** Page two
(Penal Code, § 136.2)

Document 7

The First Report (April 17, 2000) p. 1

On April 17, 2000 the Judicial Council's Center for Families, Children and the Courts issued a report which noted on page 1 that legislation *effective January 1, 2000* had amended Penal Code Section 12021(g)(2) to provide that anyone who *owns or possesses a firearm knowing he or she is prohibited from doing so by the terms of a restraining order is guilty of a public offense.*

The report also noted that the newly amended Penal Code Section 12021(g)(2) *does not apply unless either the protective order contains a notice in bold print...stating that the restrained person is prohibited from owning, possessing, or attempting to own or possess a firearm...or a court has provided actual verbal notice of the prohibition and penalties.* This report was issued three and a half (3.5) months after the California Legislature enacted Senate Bill 218 and Penal Code Section 12021(g)(2) on January 1, 2000.

Extract from Document 7

Rationale for Recommendation

Legislation effective January 1, 2000, amended Penal Code Section 12021(g) (2) to provide that anyone who *owns or possesses a firearm knowing that he or she is prohibited from doing so by the terms of a protective order is guilty of a public offense.* However, the code section *does not apply unless either the protective order contains a notice in bold print (1) stating that the person is prohibited from owning, possessing, or attempting to own or possess a firearm and (2) specifying the penalties for violating the subdivision, or a court has provided actual verbal notice of the prohibition and penalties.*

JUDICIAL COUNCIL OF CALIFORNIA
ADMINISTRATIVE OFFICE OF THE COURTS
455 Golden Gate Avenue
San Francisco, California 94102-3660

Report Summary

TO: Members of the Judicial Council

FROM: Diane Nunn, Director, Center for Families, Children and the Courts
            Tamara Abrams, Attorney, 415-865-7712
            Joshua Weinstein, Attorney, 415-865-7688

DATE: April 17, 2000

SUBJECT: Technical Revisions to Domestic Violence Forms (revise Forms
            DV-110, DV-130, and MC-220)

Issue Statement
In Senate Bill 218 (Solis) (Stats. 1999, ch. 662), the Legislature amended Penal
Code section 12021(g) to require on all protective order forms a specific notice in
bold print regarding the mandatory relinquishment of firearms by the restrained
person.

Recommendation
Staff recommends that the Judicial Council, effective July 1, 2000, revise Form
DV-110, *Order to Show Cause and Temporary Restraining Order (CLETS)
(Domestic Violence Prevention)*; Form DV-130, *Restraining Order After Hearing
(CLETS) (Domestic Violence Prevention)*; and Form MC-220, *Protective Order in
Criminal Proceeding (CLETS) (Penal Code section 136.2)*.

Rationale for Recommendation
Legislation effective January 1, 2000, amended Penal Code Section 12021(g)(2) to
provide that anyone who owns or possesses a firearm knowing that he or she is
prohibited from doing so by the terms of a protective order is guilty of a public
offense. However, the code section does not apply unless either the protective
order contains a notice in bold print (1) stating that the person is prohibited from
owning, possessing, or attempting to own or possess a firearm and (2) specifying
the penalties for violating the subdivision, or a court has provided actual verbal
notice of the prohibition and penalties. Newly amended Penal Code section

Document 8

The First Report (April 17, 2000) p. 2

The April 17, 2000 report from the Judicial Council's Center for Families, Children and the Courts noted in the first paragraph on page 2 that the newly amended Penal Code Section 12021(g)(3) requires the Judicial Council to provide a notice on the face of all protective orders warning respondents they are prohibited from *owning, possessing, purchasing, or receiving a firearm.*

The second paragraph, titled Alternative Actions Considered, noted that the Council *Staff considered creating a one-page form that could be attached to the appropriate forms* to warn the respondents they are prohibited from owning or possessing a firearm, but decided against publishing this newly required warning notice because *attaching the warning to every restraining order might be burdensome to court clerks and individuals.*

The third paragraph, titled Comments From Interested Parties, noted the press and the affected publics were never warned that the firearms prohibition notices in the Judicial Council's forms were void because *Given that the revisions referenced in this report are only technical changes to the forms, they were not distributed for public comment.*

The Judicial Council issued this report more than three and a half (3.5) months after the enactment of S.B. 218 and Penal Code Section 12021(g)(3) on January 1, 2000.

Extract from Document 8

12021(g)(3) requires the Judicial Council to provide on all protective orders notice that, among other things, the respondent is *prohibited from owning, possessing, purchasing, or receiving a firearm* while the protective order is in effect.

Alternative Actions Considered

Staff *considered creating a one-page form that could be attached to the appropriate forms.* However, *attaching the warning to every restraining order might be burdensome to court clerks and individuals.*

Comments From Interested Parties

Given that the revisions referenced in this report are only technical changes to the forms, they were not distributed for public comment.

12021(g)(3) requires the Judicial Council to provide on all protective orders notice that, among other things, the respondent is prohibited from owning, possessing, purchasing, or receiving a firearm while the protective order is in effect.

Alternative Actions Considered
Staff considered creating a one-page form that could be attached to the appropriate forms. However, attaching the warning to every restraining order might be burdensome to court clerks and individuals.

Comments From Interested Parties
Given that the revisions referenced in this report are only technical changes to the forms, they were not distributed for public comment.

The affected forms are currently being distributed to solicit public comment on other, substantive revisions for adoption effective January 1, 2001.

Implementation Requirements and Costs
The cost of implementation is limited to the photocopying of the new forms.

The text of the proposed forms is attached at pages 3 – 11.

-2-

Document 9

The First Agenda (April 24, 2000) p. 8

The April 24, 2000 Agenda for the Judicial Council's general meeting on April 28, 2000 notes on page 8 that the legal staff of the Administrative Office of the Courts (AOC) *recommends revising* the Judicial Council restraining order Forms *DV-110, DV-130,* and *DV-220* (sic) to *comply with newly amended Penal Code Section 12021(g)(3).*

This Agenda item also notes that the newly amended Penal Code Section 12021(g)(3) requires the Judicial Council to *provide notice on all protective orders that, among other things, the respondent is prohibited from owning, possessing, purchasing, or receiving a firearm.* The Judicial Council's staff made this recommendation four (4) months after the Legislature enacted Senate Bill 218 and Penal Code Section 12021(g)(3) on January 1, 2000.

Extract from Document 9

Item IV Technical Revisions to Domestic Violence Forms (revise
Forms DV-110, DV-130, and DV-220) (Action Required)

Staff Ms. Tamara Abrams

AOC staff *recommends revising* forms to *comply with newly amended Penal Code section 12021(g)(3)* requiring the Council to *provide notice on all protective orders that, among other things, the respondent is prohibited from owning, possessing, purchasing, or receiving a firearm* while the protective order is in effect.

Item 1V	**Technical Revisions to Domestic Violence Forms (revise Forms DV-110, DV-130, and DV-220) (Action Required)**
	Staff: Ms. Tamara Abrams

AOC staff recommends revising forms to comply with newly amended Penal Code section 12021 (g)(3) requiring the Council to provide notice on all protective orders that, among other things, the respondent is prohibited from owning, possessing, purchasing, or receiving a firearm while the protective order is in effect.

Item 2	**Designation of Testing Entity for Court Interpreters (Gov. Code § 68562(b)) (Action Required)**
	Staff: Mr. Joseph Wong

AOC staff recommends that Cooperative Personnel Services (CPS) be designated a testing entity for court interpreters through June 30, 2002, subject to the establishment of a mutually satisfactory agreement between the AOC and CPS.

Item 3	**Criteria for 2000–2001 Drug Court Mini-Grant Awards (Action Required)**
	Staff: Ms. Sandy Claire

The Collaborative Justice Courts Advisory Committee recommends criteria for evaluating drug court mini-grant applications for funding provided by the California Office of Criminal Justice Planning.

Item 4	**Allocation in Fiscal Years 2000–2001 and 2001–2002 for the Complex Civil Litigation Pilot Program (Action Required)**
	Staff: Ms. Alice Vilardi

The Trial Court Budget Commission recommends allocating $100,800 to continue funding the complex civil litigation pilot program in six courts at a fully annualized level.

Document 10

The First Meeting (April 28, 2000) p. 1

The Minutes for the Judicial Council's general meeting on April 28, 2000 noted on page 1 the names of the *Judicial Council members present,* including Judicial Council Chairman and California Supreme Court *Chief Justice Ronald M. George* and First District Court of Appeal Judge *Carol A. Corrigan.*

The Minutes also noted that in response to staff recommendations in the Agenda that the Judicial Council must revise the DV-110, DV-130, and MC-220 to conform to the notice requirements of Penal Code Section 12021(g)(3), *each action item on the agenda was unanimously approved on the motion made and seconded.* The Judicial Council reached this legally binding decision four (4) months after the California Legislature enacted Senate Bill 218 and Penal Code Section 12021(g)(3) on January 1, 2000.

Extract from Document 10

Judicial Council members present Chief Justice Ronald M. George; **Justices Richard D. Aldrich, Carol A. Corrigan, and Richard D. Huffman; Judges James Allen Bascue, J. Richard Couzens, Leonard P. Edwards, Donna J. Hitchens, Steven E. Jahr, Melinda A. Johnson, Ana Maria Luna, Ronald B. Robie, and Ronald L. Taylor; Mr. Michael Case and Ms. Pauline W. Gee; and advisory members Judge David John Danielsen, Mr. Ron Barrow, Mr. Stephen V. Love, Mr. Fredrich Ohlrich, and Mr. Arthur Sims.**

Except as noted, *each action item on the agenda was unanimously approved on the motion made and seconded.* (Tab letters and item numbers refer to the binder of Reports and Recommendations dated April 28, 2000, which was sent to members in advance of the meeting.

JUDICIAL COUNCIL MEETING
Minutes of April 28, 2000, Meeting

The Judicial Council of California meeting began at 9:10 a.m. on Friday, April 28, 2000, at the Administrative Office of the Courts Judicial Council Conference Center in San Francisco, California, on the call of Chief Justice Ronald M. George, Chair.

Judicial Council members present: Chief Justice Ronald M. George; Justices Richard D. Aldrich, Carol A. Corrigan, and Richard D. Huffman; Judges James Allen Bascue, J. Richard Couzens, Leonard P. Edwards, Donna J. Hitchens, Steven E. Jahr, Melinda A. Johnson, Ana Maria Luna, Ronald B. Robie, and Ronald L. Taylor; Mr. Michael Case and Ms. Pauline W. Gee; and **advisory members:** Judge David John Danielsen, Mr. Ron Barrow, Mr. Stephen V. Love, Mr. Frederick Ohlrich, and Mr. Arthur Sims.

Absent: Justice Marvin R. Baxter, Judge Paul Boland, Commissioner David L. Haet, Senator Adam B. Schiff, Assembly Member Sheila James Kuehl, Mr. John J. Collins, and Mr. Sheldon Sloan.

Others present included: Mr. William C. Vickrey; Judges Ray L. Hart, Frederick Paul Horn, and Elaine M. Watters; Ms. Beth Jay and Ms. Karen Jahr; **staff:** Ms. Jessica Fiske Bailey, Ms. Deirdre Benedict, Mr. Michael Bergeisen, Mr. Roy Blaine, Mr. James Carroll, Ms. Roma Cheadle, Ms. Eunice Collins, Mr. Blaine Corren, Ms. Lesley Duncan, Ms. Tina Hansen, Ms. Lynn Holton, Ms. Kate Howard, Ms. Melissa Johnson, Mr. Dennis Jones, Mr. Peter Kiefer, Mr. Ben McClinton, Mr. Frederick Miller, Ms. Vicki Muzny, Mr. Patrick O'Donnell, Mr. Frank Schultz, Ms. Dale Sipes, Ms. Alice Vilardi, Mr. Tony Wernert, and Mr. Jonathan Wolin; **media representatives:** Mr. Paul Elias, *The Recorder.*

Except as noted, each action item on the agenda was unanimously approved on the motion made and seconded. (Tab letters and item numbers refer to the binder of Reports and Recommendations dated April 28, 2000, which was sent to members in advance of the meeting.)

Approval of Minutes of March 17, 2000

Council action:

Justice Carol A. Corrigan moved that the Judicial Council approve the minutes of the March 17, 2000, meeting.

The motion passed.

Document 11

The First Decision (April 28, 2000) p. 14

The Minutes for the Judicial Council's general meeting on April 28, 2000 noted on page 14 that the staff of the Administrative Office of the Courts (AOC) reported to the Judicial Council that *the Legislature, in Senate Bill 218, amended Penal Code Section 12021(g) to require on all protective order forms a specific notice in bold print* warning respondents they are prohibited from *owning, possessing, purchasing, or receiving a firearm.*

The Minutes also noted under *Council action* that in response to the AOC's report, the Council voted, *effective July 1, 2000,* to revise the three forms DV-110, DV-130, and MC-220 to conform to the notice requirements of amended Penal Code Section 12021(g).

The Judicial Council reached this legally binding decision four (4) months after the Legislature enacted Senate Bill 218 and Penal Code Section 12021(g)(3) on January 1, 2000.

Extract from Document 11

Item IV
Technical Revisions to Domestic Violence Forms (revise Forms *DV-110*, *DV-130*, and *MC-220*)

AOC staff reported that *the Legislature, in Senate Bill 218, amended Penal Code section 12021(g) to require on all protective order forms a specific notice, in bold print*, regarding the mandatory relinquishment of firearms by the restrained person. The statute also requires the Judicial Council to provide on all protective orders notice that, among other things, the respondent is prohibited from *owning, possessing, purchasing, or receiving a firearm while the protective order is in effect.*

Council action
The Judicial Council, *effective July 1, 2000, revised the Order to Show Cause and Temporary Restraining Order* (CLETS) (*Domestic Violence Prevention*) (*Form DV-110), Restraining Order After Hearing (CLETS) (Domestic Violence Prevention) (Form DV-130)* and *Protective Order in Criminal Proceeding* (CLETS) (Penal Code, § 136.2) (*Form MC-220*).

Item 1V   Technical Revisions to Domestic Violence Forms (revise Forms DV-110, DV-130, and MC-220)

AOC staff reported that the Legislature, in Senate Bill 218, amended Penal Code section 12021(g) to require on all protective order forms a specific notice, in bold print, regarding the mandatory relinquishment of firearms by the restrained person. The statute also requires the Judicial Council to provide on all protective orders notice that, among other things, the respondent is prohibited from owning, possessing, purchasing, or receiving a firearm while the protective order is in effect.

Council action:

The Judicial Council, effective July 1, 2000, revised the *Order to Show Cause and Temporary Restraining Order (CLETS) (Domestic Violence Prevention)* (Form DV-110), *Restraining Order After Hearing (CLETS) (Domestic Violence Prevention)* (Form DV-130), and *Protective Order in Criminal Proceeding (CLETS) (Penal Code, § 136.2)* (Form MC-220).

ITEM 2   Designation of Testing Entity for Court Interpreters (Gov. Code, § 68562(b))

The current two-year contract with Cooperative Personnel Services to provide testing for certified and registered court interpreters will expire June 30, 2000. At present, there are no other viable testing entities with the capacity to administer the court interpreter examinations for the Judicial Council. To ensure that it can continue to offer qualifying examinations for persons interested in becoming court interpreters, the Judicial Council must designate a testing entity for the next two fiscal years. This lead time will also give universities and students time to schedule preparatory classes for upcoming test dates.

Legislation effective January 1, 1993, requires the Judicial Council to implement a comprehensive court interpreters program, including the provisional authorization of an entity to certify interpreters pending its approval of more permanent testing entities.

Council action:

The Judicial Council:
1. Designated Cooperative Personnel Services (CPS) as a testing entity to certify court interpreters, effective July 1, 2000, through June 30, 2002, subject to the establishment of a mutually satisfactory agreement between the Administrative Office of the Courts and CPS; and
2. Delegated future selection of testing entities to the Administrative Director of the Courts.

Chapter 6
The Void Restriction

Document 12

Form DV-110 (New Jan. 1, 1999) p. 2

The Judicial Council published the domestic violence temporary restraining order Form DV-110 (*Order to Show Cause and Temporary Restraining Order*) on January 1, 1999, one (1) year before the California Legislature enacted Senate Bill 218 and Family Code Section 6389(c) on January 1, 2000.

The Firearm Restriction notice on page 2 of this new form violated due process by ordering the respondents to give up their private property, their firearms, before they had an opportunity to appear and be heard at a noticed hearing in open court.

When the Judicial Council republished this January 1, 1999 edition of the DV-110 on January 1, 2000, the Firearm Restriction notice violated due process and the notice requirements of the newly amended Family Code Section 6389(c) by ordering respondents to *give up any firearm* in their *possession or control* before they had an opportunity to appear and be heard at a noticed hearing in open court, and by failing to refer to the presence or the absence of the respondent at that noticed court hearing.

Extract from Document 12

7. FIREARM RESTRICTION

The restrained person is ordered to *give up any firearm* in or subject to his or her immediate *possession or control* within

a. *24 hours after issuance* of this order

b. *48 hours after service* of this order

c. other (*specify*)

5. b. ☐ must immediately move from *(address)*:

and take only personal clothing and effects needed until the hearing.

c. ☐ The restrained person shall stay at least *(specify)*:   **yards** away from the following persons and places.
(Addresses not required.)
(1) ☐ Person seeking the order
(2) ☐ The other protected persons listed in item 4b
(3) ☐ Residence of person seeking the order
(4) ☐ Place of work of person seeking the order
(5) ☐ The children's school or place of child care
(6) ☐ Protected person's vehicle *(specify)*:
(7) ☐ Other *(specify)*:

d. ☐ except for peaceful contacts related to court ordered visitation of the minor children.

6. ☐ **CUSTODY AND VISITATION ORDERS ARE SET FORTH IN** *CHILD CUSTODY AND VISITATION ORDER ATTACHMENT* **(FORM 1296.31A).**

7. ☐ **FIREARM RESTRICTION**
The restrained person is ordered to give up any firearm in or subject to his or her immediate possession or control within
☐ 24 hours after issuance of this order
☐ 48 hours after service of this order
☐ other *(specify)*:

Any firearms should be surrendered to the control of local law enforcement. **The restrained person shall file a receipt with the court showing compliance with this order within 72 hours of receiving this order.**

8. ☐ **PROPERTY CONTROL**
a. ☐ The protected person is given exclusive temporary use, control, and possession of the following property pending the hearing:

b. ☐ The restrained person is ordered to make the following payments while the order is in effect:
        Debt   Amount of payment   Pay to   Due date

c. ☐ The protected person   ☐ The restrained person   is restrained from transferring, borrowing against, selling, hiding, or in any way disposing of any real or personal property, whether community, quasi-community, or separate, except in the ordinary course of business or for the necessities of life.
d. ☐ The protected person   ☐ The restrained person   shall notify the other of any proposed extraordinary expenditures and shall account to the court for all extraordinary expenditures.

9. ☐ **OTHER ORDERS** *(specify)*:

(Continued on page three)

DV-110 [New January 1, 1999]   **ORDER TO SHOW CAUSE AND TEMPORARY RESTRAINING ORDER**   Page two of four
(CLETS) (Domestic Violence Prevention)

45

Document 13

Form DV-110 (Rev. July 1, 2000) p. 2

The Judicial Council revised the domestic violence temporary restraining order Form DV-110 (*Order to Show Cause and Temporary Restraining Order*) on July 1, 2000, six (6) months after the California Legislature enacted Senate Bill 218 and Family Code Section 6389(c) on January 1, 2000.

      The Firearm Restriction on page 2 of this revision violated due process and the notice requirements of the newly amended Family Code Section 6389(c) by ordering the respondents to *give up any firearms* in their *possession or control* before they had an opportunity to appear and be heard at a noticed hearing in open court, and by failing to refer to the presence or the absence of the respondent at that noticed court hearing.

Extract from Document 13

7. FIREARM RESTRICTION

The restrained person is ordered to *give up any firearm* in or subject to his or her immediate *possession or control* within

a. *24 hours after issuance* of this order

b. *48 hours after service* of this order
c. other (*specify*)

PERSON SEEKING ORDER (name):	CASE NUMBER:
PERSON TO BE RESTRAINED (name):	

5. b. ☐ must immediately move from (address):

and take only personal clothing and effects needed until the hearing.

c. ☐ The restrained person shall stay at least (specify): _____ yards away from the following persons and places. (Addresses not required.)

    (1) ☐ Person seeking the order

    (2) ☐ The other protected persons listed in item 4b

    (3) ☐ Residence of person seeking the order

    (4) ☐ Place of work of person seeking the order

    (5) ☐ The children's school or place of child care

    (6) ☐ Protected person's vehicle (specify):

    (7) ☐ Other (specify):

d. ☐ except for peaceful contacts related to court ordered visitation of the minor children.

6. ☐ CUSTODY AND VISITATION ORDERS ARE SET FORTH IN CHILD CUSTODY AND VISITATION ORDER ATTACHMENT (FORM 1296.31A).

7. ☐ FIREARM RESTRICTION

The restrained person is ordered to give up any firearm in or subject to his or her immediate possession or control within

a. ☐ 24 hours after issuance of this order

b. ☐ 48 hours after service of this order

c. ☐ other (specify):

Any firearms should be surrendered to the control of local law enforcement. **The restrained person shall file a receipt with the court showing compliance with this order within 72 hours of receiving this order.**

8. ☐ PROPERTY CONTROL

a. ☐ The protected person is given exclusive temporary use, control, and possession of the following property pending the hearing:

b. ☐ The restrained person is ordered to make the following payments while the order is in effect:

Debt	Amount of payment	Pay to	Due date

c. ☐ The protected person ☐ The restrained person is restrained from transferring, borrowing against, selling, hiding, or in any way disposing of any real or personal property, whether community, quasi-community, or separate, except in the ordinary course of business or for the necessities of life.

d. ☐ The protected person ☐ The restrained person shall notify the other of any proposed extraordinary expenditures and shall account to the court for all extraordinary expenditures.

9. ☐ OTHER ORDERS (specify):

(Continued on page three)

ORDER TO SHOW CAUSE AND TEMPORARY RESTRAINING ORDER (CLETS) (Domestic Violence Prevention)

Document 14

Form DV-110 (Rev. Jan. 1, 2001) p. 2

The Judicial Council revised the domestic violence temporary restraining order Form DV-110 (*Order to Show Cause and Temporary Restraining Order*) again on January 1, 2001, one (1) year after the California Legislature enacted Senate Bill 218 and Family Code Section 6389(c) on January 1, 2000.

The Firearm Relinquishment notice on page 2 of this revision conformed to the notice requirements of amended Family Code Section 6389(c) by referring to the presence or the absence of the restraining order respondent at a preceding noticed hearing in open court with two parenthetical phrases: *If restrained person is present at hearing* and *If restrained person is not present at hearing*.

Extract from Document 14

7. FIREARM RELINQUISHMENT

The restrained person must surrender to local law enforcement or sell to a licensed gun dealer any firearm in or subject to his or her immediate possession or control within

a. 24 hours after issuance of this order (*If restrained person is present at hearing*).

b. 48 hours after service of this order (*If restrained person is not present at hearing*).

c. other (*specify*)

5. b. ☐ must immediately move from (address):

and take only personal clothing and effects needed until the hearing.

c. ☐ The restrained person shall stay at least (specify): _____ yards away from the following persons and places. (Addresses not required.)

    (1) ☐ Person seeking the order
    (2) ☐ The other protected persons listed in item 4b
    (3) ☐ Residence of person seeking the order
    (4) ☐ Place of work of person seeking the order
    (5) ☐ The children's school or place of child care
    (6) ☐ Protected person's vehicle
    (7) ☐ Other (specify):

d. ☐ except for peaceful contacts related to court ordered visitation of the minor children.

6. ☐ CUSTODY AND VISITATION ORDERS ARE SET FORTH IN *CHILD CUSTODY AND VISITATION ORDER ATTACHMENT* (FORM 1296.31A).

7. ☐ FIREARM RELINQUISHMENT
The restrained person must surrender to local law enforcement or sell to a licensed gun dealer any firearm in or subject to his or her immediate possession or control within

a. ☐ 24 hours after issuance of this order (if restrained person is present at hearing).
b. ☐ 48 hours after service of this order (if restrained person is not present at hearing).
c. ☐ other (specify):

The restrained person shall file a receipt with the court showing compliance with this order within 72 hours of receiving this order.

8. ☐ PROPERTY CONTROL
a. ☐ The protected person is given exclusive temporary use, control, and possession of the following property pending the hearing:

b. ☐ The restrained person is ordered to make the following payments while the order is in effect:

Debt	Amount of payment	Pay to	Due date

c. ☐ The protected person ☐ The restrained person is restrained from transferring, borrowing against, selling, hiding, or in any way disposing of any real or personal property, whether community, quasi-community, or separate, except in the ordinary course of business or for the necessities of life.

d. ☐ The protected person ☐ The restrained person shall notify the other of any proposed extraordinary expenditures and shall account to the court for all extraordinary expenditures.

9. ☐ RECORDING OF PROHIBITED COMMUNICATIONS
The protected person may record any prohibited communications made to him or her by the restrained person.

10. ☐ OTHER ORDERS (specify):

(Continued on page three)

Document 15

Form DV-130 (New Jan. 1, 1999) p. 2

The Judicial Council published the domestic violence post-hearing restraining order Form DV-130 (*Order After Hearing*) on January 1, 1999, one (1) year before the California Legislature enacted Senate Bill 218 and Family Code Section 6389(c) on January 1, 2000.

The Firearm Relinquishment notice on page 2 of this newly published Judicial Council restraining order form violated Constitutional due process guarantees by ordering the restraining order respondents to give up their private property, their firearms, before they had an opportunity to appear and be heard at a noticed hearing in open court.

When the Judicial Council republished this January 1, 1999 edition of the DV-130 on January 1, 2000, the Firearm Relinquishment notice on page 2 still violated due process and the notice requirements of newly amended Family Code Section 6389(c) by ordering the respondents to *give up any firearm* in their *possession or control* before they had an opportunity to appear and be heard at a noticed court hearing, and by failing to refer to the presence or the absence of the restraining order respondent at that court hearing.

Extract from Document 15

8. FIREARM RELINQUISHMENT

The restrained person is ordered t o *give up any firearm* in his or her immediate *possession or control* within

***24 hours after issuance* of this order**

***48 hours after service* of this order**
other (specify)

PROTECTED PERSON *(name)*:	CASE NUMBER:
RESTRAINED PERSON *(name)*:	

> *Read this order carefully. Taking or concealing a child in violation of this order may be a felony and punishable by confinement in state prison, a fine, or both. Any person subject to a restraining order is prohibited from purchasing or attempting to purchase, receiving or attempting to receive, or otherwise obtaining a firearm. Possession of a firearm while subject to this order may be a felony under federal law punishable by up to ten (10) years in prison and a $25,000 fine.*

5. ☐ **CHILD CUSTODY AND VISITATION**

The custody and visitation of the minor children is ordered as set forth in the attached forms, which are incorporated herein and made an operative part of this order. Peaceful contacts shall be allowed related to court-ordered visitation.

☐ *Child Custody and Visitation Order Attachment* (form 1296.31A)
☐ *Supervised Visitation Order* (form 1296.31A(1))
☐ Other *(specify)*:

6. ☐ **CHILD SUPPORT**

Child support for the minor children shall be ordered as set forth in the attached forms, which are incorporated herein and made an operative part of this order.

☐ *Child Support Information and Order Attachment* (form 1296.31B)
☐ Other *(specify)*:

7. ☐ **ADDITIONAL ORDERS**

Additional orders relating to property control, debt payment, attorney fees, restitution, counseling and/or other orders are set forth in the attached forms, which are incorporated herein and made an operative part of this order.

☐ *Domestic Violence Miscellaneous Orders Attachment* (form 1296.31E)
☐ Other *(specify)*:

8. ☐ **FIREARM RELINQUISHMENT**

The restrained person is ordered to give up any firearm in or subject to his or her immediate possession or control within

☐ 24 hours after issuance of this order
☐ 48 hours after service of this order
☐ other *(specify)*:

Any firearms should be surrendered to the control of local law enforcement, sold to a licensed gun dealer, or relinquished pursuant to Family Code section 6389(l). **The restrained person shall file a receipt with the court showing compliance with this order within 72 hours of receiving this order.**

9. ☐ The restrained person is ordered to participate in a certified batterer's program for 12 months at that party's expense with the results of attendance and completion to be provided to the court.

10. ☐ Fees for service of this order by law enforcement are waived.

11. ☐ A copy of this order shall be delivered by the protected person to the law enforcement agency having jurisdiction over the residence of the protected person, who shall provide information to assist in identifying the restrained person. Proof of service of this order on the restrained person shall also be provided to law enforcement unless the order shows the restrained person was present in court. The law enforcement agency having jurisdiction over the plaintiff's residence is *(name and address of agency)*:

(Continued on page three)

Document 16

Form DV-130 (Rev. July 1, 2000) p. 2

The Judicial Council revised the domestic violence post-hearing restraining order Form DV-130 (*Order After Hearing*) on July 1, 2000, six (6) months after the Legislature enacted Senate Bill 218 and Family Code Section 6389(c) on January 1, 2000.

The Firearm Relinquishment Notice on page 2 of this revision violated due process and the notice requirements of the newly amended Family Code Section 6389(c) by ordering the respondents to *give up any firearm* in their *possession or control* before they had an opportunity to appear and be heard at a noticed court hearing, and by failing to refer to the presence or the absence of the respondent at that noticed hearing in open court.

Extract from Document 16

8. FIREARM RELINQUISHMENT

The restrained person is ordered to *give up any firearm* in his or her immediate *possession or control* within

a. *24 hours after issuance* of this order

b. *48 hours after service* of this order

c. other (*specify*)

> *Read this order carefully. Taking or concealing a child in violation of this order may be a felony and punishable by confinement in state prison, a fine, or both. Any person subject to a restraining order is prohibited from owning, possessing, purchasing or attempting to purchase, receiving or attempting to receive, or otherwise obtaining a firearm. Possession of a firearm while subject to this order may be a felony under federal law punishable by up to ten (10) years in prison and a $25,000 fine.*

5. ☐ **CHILD CUSTODY AND VISITATION**

The custody and visitation of the minor children is ordered as set forth in the attached forms, which are incorporated herein and made an operative part of this order. Peaceful contacts shall be allowed related to court-ordered visitation.

a. ☐ *Child Custody and Visitation Order Attachment* (form 1296.31A)
b. ☐ *Supervised Visitation Order* (form 1296.31A(1))
c. ☐ Other *(specify)*:

6. ☐ **CHILD SUPPORT**

Child support for the minor children shall be ordered as set forth in the attached forms, which are incorporated herein and made an operative part of this order.

a. ☐ *Child Support Information and Order Attachment* (form 1296.31B)
b. ☐ Other *(specify)*:

7. ☐ **ADDITIONAL ORDERS**

Additional orders relating to property control, debt payment, attorney fees, restitution, counseling and/or other orders are set forth in the attached forms, which are incorporated herein and made an operative part of this order.

a. ☐ *Domestic Violence Miscellaneous Orders Attachment* (form 1296.31E)
b. ☐ Other *(specify)*:

8. **FIREARM RELINQUISHMENT**

The restrained person is ordered to give up any firearm in or subject to his or her immediate possession or control within

a. ☐ **24 hours after issuance of this order**
b. ☐ **48 hours after service of this order**
c. ☐ **other** *(specify)*:

Any firearms should be surrendered to the control of local law enforcement, sold to a licensed gun dealer, or relinquished pursuant to Family Code section 6389. **The restrained person shall file a receipt with the court showing compliance with this order within 72 hours of receiving this order.**

9. ☐ The restrained person is ordered to participate in a certified batterer's program for 12 months at that party's expense with the results of attendance and completion to be provided to the court.

10. ☐ Fees for service of this order by law enforcement are waived.

11. ☐ A copy of this order shall be delivered by the protected person to the law enforcement agency having jurisdiction over the residence of the protected person, who shall provide information to assist in identifying the restrained person. Proof of service of this order on the restrained person shall also be provided to law enforcement unless the order shows the restrained person was present in court. The law enforcement agency having jurisdiction over the plaintiff's residence is *(name and address of agency)*:

(Continued on page three)

DV-130 [Rev. July 1, 2000]	**RESTRAINING ORDER AFTER HEARING (CLETS)** **(Domestic Violence Prevention)**	Page two of three

53

Document 17

Form DV-130 (Rev. Jan. 1, 2001) p. 2

The Judicial Council revised the domestic violence post-hearing restraining order Form DV-130 (*Restraining Order After Hearing*) again on January 1, 2001, one (1) year after the Legislature enacted Senate Bill 218 and Family Code Section 6389(c) on January 1, 2000.

The Mandatory Firearm Relinquishment Notice on page 2 of this revision conformed to the notice requirements of amended Family Code Section 6389(c) by referring to the presence or the absence of the restraining order respondent at a prior noticed court hearing with two parenthetical phrases: *If restrained person is present at hearing* and *If restrained person is not present at hearing*.

Extract from Document 17

8. MANDATORY FIREARM RELINQUISHMENT

The restrained person must surrender to local law enforcement or sell to a licensed gun dealer any firearm in or subject to his or her immediate possession or control within

a. 24 hours after issuance of this order (*If restrained person is present at hearing*)

b. 48 hours after service of this order (*If restrained person is not present at hearing*)

c. other (*specify*)

PROTECTED PERSON (name):	CASE NUMBER:
RESTRAINED PERSON (name):	

4. c. *(Continued)*
      (5) ☐ the children's school or place of child care
      (6) ☐ protected person's vehicle
      (7) ☐ other *(specify)*:

> *Read this order carefully. Taking or concealing a child in violation of this order may be a felony and punishable by confinement in state prison, a fine, or both.*

5. ☐ **CHILD CUSTODY AND VISITATION**
    The custody and visitation of the minor children is ordered as set forth in the attached forms, which are incorporated herein and made an operative part of this order. Peaceful contacts shall be allowed related to court-ordered visitation.
    a. ☐ *Child Custody and Visitation Order Attachment* (form 1296.31A)
    b. ☐ *Supervised Visitation Order* (form 1296.31A(1))
    c. ☐ Other *(specify)*:

6. ☐ **CHILD SUPPORT**
    Child support for the minor children shall be ordered as set forth in the attached forms, which are incorporated herein and made an operative part of this order.
    a. ☐ *Child Support Information and Order Attachment* (form 1296.31B)
    b. ☐ Other *(specify)*:

7. ☐ **ADDITIONAL ORDERS**
    Additional orders relating to property control, debt payment, attorney fees, restitution, counseling and/or other orders are set forth in the attached forms, which are incorporated herein and made an operative part of this order.
    a. ☐ *Domestic Violence Miscellaneous Orders Attachment* (form 1296.31E)
    b. ☐ Other *(specify)*:

8. **MANDATORY FIREARM RELINQUISHMENT**
    The restrained person must surrender to local law enforcement or sell to a licensed gun dealer any firearm in or subject to his or her immediate possession or control within
    a. ☐ **24 hours after issuance of this order (if restrained person is present at hearing).**
    b. ☐ **48 hours after service of this order (if restrained person is not present at hearing).**
    c. ☐ **other *(specify)*:**

    The restrained person shall file a receipt with the court showing compliance with this order within 72 hours of receiving this order.

9. ☐ **RECORDING OF PROHIBITED COMMUNICATIONS**
    The protected person may record any prohibited communication made to him or her by the restrained person.

10. ☐ The restrained person is ordered to participate in a certified batterer's program for 12 months at that party's expense with the results of attendance and completion to be provided to the court.

11. ☐ Fees for service of this order by law enforcement are waived.

(Continued on page three)

DV-130 [Rev. January 1, 2001]
RESTRAINING ORDER AFTER HEARING (CLETS)
(Domestic Violence Prevention)
Page two of three

55

Document 18

Form MC-220 (Rev. July 1, 2000) p. 1

The Judicial Council revised the criminal court restraining order Form MC-220 (*Protective Order in Criminal Proceeding*) on July 1, 2000, six (6) months after the California Legislature enacted Senate Bill 218 and Family Code Section 6389(c) on January 1, 2000.

The firearm prohibition notice on page 1 of this revision violated due process and the notice requirements of the newly amended Family Code Section 6389(c) by ordering respondents to *give up any firearm* in their *possession or control* before they had an opportunity to appear and be heard at a noticed hearing in an open court, and by failing to refer to the presence or absence of the restraining order respondent at that noticed hearing.

Extract from Document 18

GOOD CAUSE APPEARING, THE COURT ORDERS that the above named defendant

f. shall *give up any firearm* in or subject to his or her immediate *possession or control* within

(1) *24 hours after issuance* of this order

(2) *48 hours after service* of this order

(3) other (*specify*)

NAME OF COURT AND DISTRICT, BRANCH, OR DIVISION, IF ANY:	*FOR COURT USE ONLY*

PEOPLE OF THE STATE OF CALIFORNIA

vs.

DEFENDANT:

PROTECTIVE ORDER IN CRIMINAL PROCEEDING (CLETS) (Penal Code, § 136.2) ☐ **MODIFICATION**	CASE NUMBER:

THIS ORDER TAKES PRECEDENCE OVER ANY PRIOR COURT ORDER

PERSON TO BE RESTRAINED *(Name)*: _____

Sex: ☐ M ☐ F Ht.: _____ Wt.: _____ Hair Color: _____ Eye Color: ___ Race: ___ Age: ___ Date of Birth: _____

☐ The defendant is a peace officer with _____ Department.

1. This proceeding was heard
   on *(date)*: _____ at *(time)*: _____ in Dept.: _____ Room: _____
   by judicial officer *(name)*: _____

2. ☐ Defendant was personally present at the court hearing, and no additional proof of service of the restraining order is required.

3. **GOOD CAUSE APPEARING, THE COURT ORDERS** that the above-named defendant
   a. ☐ shall not annoy, harass, strike, threaten, sexually assault, batter, stalk, destroy personal property of, or otherwise disturb the peace of the protected persons named below.
   b. ☐ shall have no personal, telephonic, or written contact with the protected persons named below.
   c. ☐ shall have no contact with the protected persons named below through a third party, except an attorney of record.
   d. ☐ shall not come within _____ yards of the protected persons named below.
   e. ☐ shall not attempt to or actually prevent or dissuade any victim or witness from attending a hearing or testifying or making a report to any law enforcement agency or person.
   f. ☐ **shall give up any firearm in or subject to his or her immediate possession or control within**
      (1) ☐ **24 hours after issuance of this order**
      (2) ☐ **48 hours after service of this order**
      (3) ☐ **other *(specify)*:**

   Any firearms should be surrendered to the control of local law enforcement. **The restrained person shall file a receipt with the court showing compliance with this order within 72 hours of receiving this order.**

4. NAMES OF PROTECTED PERSONS:

5. Other orders *(specify)*:

6. This order expires on *(specify date)*:
   If no date is listed, this order expires three years from the date of issuance.

Date: _____

JUDICIAL OFFICER   Department/Division: _____

(See warnings on reverse)

WEST GROUP

Form Approved for Optional Use
 Judicial Council of California
 MC-220 [Rev. July 1, 2000] **PROTECTIVE ORDER IN CRIMINAL PROCEEDING (CLETS)**
 (Penal Code, § 136.2)   Penal Code, §§ 136.2, 166

(Distribution: original to file; 1 copy to each protected person; 1 copy to defendant; 1 copy to prosecutor; 1 copy to law enforcement)

Document 19

Form MC-220 (Rev. Jan. 1, 2001) p. 1

The Judicial Council revised the criminal court restraining order Form MC-220 (*Protective Order in Criminal Proceeding*) again on January 1, 2001, one (1) year after the California Legislature enacted Senate Bill 218 and Family Code Section 6389(c) on January 1, 2000.

The firearms relinquishment notice on page 1 of this revision violated due process and the notice requirements of Family Code Section 6389(c) by ordering respondents to *surrender* or *sell* any firearm *in or subject to his or her immediate possession or control* before they had an opportunity to appear and be heard at a noticed hearing, and by failing to refer to the presence or absence of the respondent at that noticed hearing. Nevertheless, the Judicial Council repeatedly republished this void January 1, 2001 revision of the Form MC-220 for the next six (6) years, and the California Courts continued to issue their protective orders on this void form until the MC-220 was discontinued on January 1, 2007.

Extract from Document 19

GOOD CAUSE APPEARING, THE COURT ORDERS

3. The above named defendant

c. must *surrender* to local law enforcement or *sell* to a licensed gun dealer any firearm *in or subject to his or her immediate possession or control* within

(1) *24 hours after issuance* of this order

(2) *48 hours after service* of this order

(3) other (*specify*)

NAME OF COURT AND DISTRICT, BRANCH, OR DIVISION, IF ANY:	FOR COURT USE ONLY
PEOPLE OF THE STATE OF CALIFORNIA vs. DEFENDANT:	

| **PROTECTIVE ORDER IN CRIMINAL PROCEEDING (CLETS)**
(Penal Code, § 136.2)
☐ ORDER PENDING TRIAL   ☐ MODIFICATION
☐ ORDER POST TRIAL PROBATION CONDITION | CASE NUMBER: |

THIS ORDER TAKES PRECEDENCE OVER ANY CONFLICTING COURT ORDER

PERSON TO BE RESTRAINED *(Name):* _____

Sex: ☐ M ☐ F   Ht.: _____ Wt.: _____ Hair Color: _____ Eye Color: _____ Race: _____ Age: _____ Date of Birth: _____

☐ The defendant is a peace officer with _____ Department.

1. This proceeding was heard
   on *(date):*   at *(time):*   in Dept.:   Room:
   by judicial officer *(name):*
2. ☐ Defendant was personally present at the court hearing, and no additional proof of service of the restraining order is required.

GOOD CAUSE APPEARING, THE COURT ORDERS

3. The above-named defendant
   a. shall not annoy, harass, strike, threaten, sexually assault, batter, stalk, destroy personal property of, or otherwise disturb the peace of the protected persons named below.
   b. shall not attempt to or actually prevent or dissuade any victim or witness from attending a hearing or testifying or making a report to any law enforcement agency or person.
   c. **must surrender to local law enforcement or sell to licensed gun dealer any firearm in or subject to his or her immediate possession or control within**
      (1) ☐ 24 hours after issuance of this order
      (2) ☐ 48 hours after service of this order
      (3) ☐ other *(specify):*

      The restrained person shall file a receipt with the court showing compliance with this order within 72 hours of receiving this order.
   d. ☐ shall have no personal, telephonic, or written contact with the protected persons named below.
   e. ☐ shall have no contact with the protected persons named below through a third party, except an attorney of record.
   f. ☐ shall not come within _____ yards of the protected persons named below.
   g. ☐ shall have peaceful contact with the protected persons named above for court-ordered visitation as ordered in prior or subsequent Family Court and Juvenile Court orders as an exemption to the "no contact" and "stay away" provisions of this order.
4. ☐ The protected person may record any prohibited communications made to him or her by the restrained person.
5. NAMES OF PROTECTED PERSONS:

6. Other orders including stay-away orders from specific locations:

7. This order expires on *(specify date):*
   If no date is listed, this order expires three years from the date of issuance.

Date: _____

_____
JUDICIAL OFFICER   Department/Division:

(See warnings on reverse)

Form Adopted for Mandatory Use
Judicial Council of California
MC-220 [Rev. January 1, 2001] **PROTECTIVE ORDER IN CRIMINAL PROCEEDING (CLETS)**
(Penal Code, § 136.2)   Penal Code, §§ 136.2, 166
Form Approved by
Department of Justice

(Distribution: original to file; 1 copy to each protected person; 1 copy to defendant; 1 copy to prosecutor; 1 copy to law enforcement)

Document 20

The Second Report (Oct. 5, 2000) p. 5

On October 5, 2000 the Judicial Council's Family and Juvenile Law Advisory Committee issued a second report, which noted on page 5 that, among other things, the Judicial Council was required to revise the domestic violence restraining order forms DV-110 and DV-130, *Pursuant to New Legislation.*

The concluding sentence of the Issue Statement in this report noted *the proposal addresses the issue of firearm relinquishment upon the issuance of a temporary restraining order.*

The Judicial Council issued this Advisory Committee report ten (10) months after the California Legislature enacted Senate Bill 218 on January 1, 2000

Extract from Document 20

SUBJECT *Domestic Violence* and Family Law Support *Forms* and UCCJEA and Related Forms–*Technical Changes Pursuant to New Legislation* and Public Comment (*revise Forms* DV-100, *DV-110*, DV-120, *DV-130*, DV-140, DV-150, 1281, 1282, 1296.60, 1296.80, 1296.81, MC-150, 1296.31B, 1296.31C, GC-210 (*Action Required*).

Issue Statement

The proposal responds to three separate issues.... Finally, *the proposal addresses the issue of firearm relinquishment upon the issuance of a temporary restraining order.*

JUDICIAL COUNCIL OF CALIFORNIA
ADMINISTRATIVE OFFICE OF THE COURTS
455 Golden Gate Avenue
San Francisco, California 94102-3660

Report

TO: Members of the Judicial Council

FROM: Family and Juvenile Law Advisory Committee
              Tamara Abrams, Attorney, 415/865-7712
              Michael Fischer, Senior Attorney, 415/865-7685
              Bonnie Hough, Senior Attorney, 415/865-7668
              Ruth McCreight, Senior Attorney, 415/865-7666

DATE: October 5, 2000

SUBJECT: Domestic Violence and Family Law Support Forms and UCCJEA and
              Related Forms — Technical Changes Pursuant to New Legislation and
              Public Comment (revise Forms DV-100, DV-110, DV-120, DV-130,
              DV-140, DV-150, 1281, 1282, 1296.60, 1296.80, 1296.81, MC-150,
              1296.31B, 1296.31C, GC-210)
              <u>(Action Required)</u>

Issue Statement

The proposal responds to three separate issues. First, the proposal makes technical
changes to a variety of forms to reflect the adoption of the Uniform Child Custody
Jurisdiction and Enforcement Act pursuant to Family Code section 3400 et seq.
Second, the proposal makes technical improvements to two family law support
forms. Third, the proposal makes technical and substantive changes to the domestic
violence restraining order forms pursuant to newly added Penal Code section 633.6.
Under the amended section, a judicial officer may permit a victim of domestic
violence to request an order to record any prohibited communication made to him or
her by the restrained person. The statute requires the Judicial Council to amend its
domestic violence forms accordingly. The proposal also makes clarifying changes in
response to comments from law enforcement. Finally, the proposal addresses the
issue of firearm relinquishment upon the issuance of a temporary restraining order.

Recommendation

The Family and Juvenile Law Advisory Committee recommends that the Judicial
Council, effective January 1, 2001:

1. Revise Forms 1281, *Petition (Family Law)*; 1282, *Response (Family Law)*;
   1296.60, *Petition to Establish Parental Relationship (Uniform Parentage)*;
   1296.80, *Petition for Custody and Support of Minor Children*; 1296.81, *Response*

5

61

Document 21

The Second Report (Oct. 5, 2000) p. 9

The October 5, 2000 report from the Judicial Council's Family and Juvenile Law Advisory Committee noted on page 9 that the Firearm Restriction notice in the Judicial Council restraining order forms DV-110 and DV-130 *also refers to a noticed hearing.*

The report also noted that although Family Code 6389(c) specified the time for firearm relinquishment if the respondent *is present* at a noticed hearing or *not present* at such a hearing, section (c) *does not address relinquishment in the situation where a temporary restraining order is issued without notice and without a hearing.*

The Judicial Council issued this report ten (10) months after the California Legislature enacted Senate Bill 218 on January 1, 2000.

Extract from Document 21

Furthermore, section (c), which sets out the deadlines by which firearms must be relinquished, *also refers to a noticed hearing.* If the respondent is present at a duly noticed hearing, the court shall order the respondent to relinquish any firearm ... within 24 hours of the order.... If the respondent is not present at the hearing, the respondent shall relinquish the firearm within 48 hours after being served with the order. (Fam. Code § 6389(c), italics added.)

Thus, *section (c)* specifies the time for relinquishment if the respondent is present at a noticed hearing or not present at such a hearing, but it *does not address relinquishment in the situation where a temporary restraining order is issued without notice and without a hearing.*

In many, if not most, cases, the person seeking the order is not present in court while the judicial officer reviews the application and proposed order. After review, the judicial officer may grant the temporary orders, which remain in effect until the hearing, usually scheduled within three weeks. The protected person is then responsible for ensuring that the restrained person is provided with notice of the hearing.

Analysis. Family Code section 6389(a) explicitly prohibits any person "subject to a protective order, as defined in Section 6218" from owning, possessing, purchasing, or receiving a firearm. Family Code section 6218 includes protective orders issued ex parte as well as after notice and a hearing.

This section can be interpreted to require the court to order firearms relinquished as soon as it issues any domestic violence restraining order, regardless of whether the order was issued with notice to the restrained person. However, the next two sections of the statute confuse the issue. Family Code section 6389(b) requires the Judicial Council to include a notice on all forms requesting a protective order that, *at the hearing for a protective order*, the respondent shall be ordered to relinquish possession or control of firearms. Because most temporary restraining orders are issued without notice or a hearing, it is unclear at what point in the restraining order process the Legislature intended the court to require firearm relinquishment.

Furthermore, section (c), which sets out the deadlines by which firearms must be relinquished, also refers to a noticed hearing: *If the respondent is present at a duly noticed hearing*, the court shall order the respondent to relinquish any firearm … within 24 hours of the order....*If the respondent is not present at the hearing*, the respondent shall relinquish the firearm within 48 hours after being served with the order. (Fam. Code §6389(c), italics added.)

Thus, section (c) specifies the time for relinquishment if the respondent is present at a noticed hearing or not present at such a hearing, but it does not address relinquishment in the situation where a temporary restraining order is issued without notice and without a hearing.

Argument that firearm relinquishment is required only after a noticed hearing.
There appears to be some inconsistency between section (a) and sections (b) and (c) of Family Code section 6389. In cases of inconsistency between statutory provisions, under principles of statutory construction the specific statute prevails over a general one when the two sections cannot be reconciled. (In re Ricardo A. (1995) 32 Cal.App.4th 1190, review den. May 17, 1995). Therefore, because sections (b) and (c) are more specific about when and under what circumstances firearms are to be relinquished, and because they cannot be reconciled with the explicit provision of section (a), sections (b) and (c) are controlling.

9

Document 22

The Second Agenda (Oct. 27, 2000) p. 11

The Agenda for the Judicial Council's October 27, 2000 general meeting noted on page 11 that the Judicial Council's Family and Juvenile Law Advisory Committee recommended revising the *Domestic Violence and Family Law Support Forms,* including the restraining order Forms *DV-110* and *DV-130,* to *conform to recent statutory changes regarding firearm relinquishment."*

The Judicial Council issued these Advisory Committee recommendations ten (10) months after the California Legislature enacted Senate Bill 218 on January 1, 2000.

Extract from Document 22

Item 6
8:55-9:10 a.m.

Domestic Violence and Family Law Support Forms **(revise Forms DV-100,** ***DV-110,*** **DV-120,** ***DV-130,*** **DV-140, DV-150, 1281, 1282, 1296.60, 1296.80, 1296.81, MC-150, 1296.31B, 1296.31C, and GC-210) (Action Required)**

The Family and Juvenile Law Advisory Committee recommends revising forms to ***conform to recent statutory changes regarding firearm relinquishment*** **and recording of prohibited communications.**

Item 6
8:55–9:10 a.m.

Domestic Violence and Family Law Support Forms (revise Forms DV-100, DV-110, DV-120, DV-130, DV-140, DV-150, 1281, 1282, 1296.60, 1296.80, 1296.81, MC-150, 1296.31B, 1296.31C, and GC-210) (Action Required)

The Family and Juvenile Law Advisory Committee recommends revising forms to conform to recent statutory changes regarding firearm relinquishment and recording of prohibited communications.

Presentation (5 minutes)
Speakers: Ms. Tamara Abrams
                     Ms. Diane Nunn
Discussion/Council Action (10 minutes)

Item 7
9:10–9:25 a.m.

Requesting Psychotropic Medication of Juveniles (adopt Cal. Rules of Court, rule 1432.5 and Form JV-220) (Action Required)

The Family and Juvenile Law Advisory Committee recommends adopting a new rule and form to conform with recent statutory changes regarding orders concerning dependent children and psychotropic medication.

Presentation (5 minutes)
Speakers: Mr. John Sweeney
                     Ms. Diane Nunn
Discussion/Council Action (10 minutes)

Item 8
9:25–9:40 a.m.

Implementation of Proposition 21 and Senate Bill 334 (amend Cal. Rules of Court, rules 1430, 1431, 1470, 1480, and 1483; revise Form JV-710; and adopt Forms JV-615, JV-635, JV-750, and JV-751) (Action Required)

The Criminal Law and Family and Juvenile Law Advisory Committees recommend changes to rules and forms to implement Proposition 21, the "juvenile crime initiative" and recent statutory changes in the administration of justice in delinquency cases.

Presentation (10 minutes)
Speakers: Ms. Diane Nunn
                     Mr. Joshua Weinstein
                     Ms. Audrey Evje
Discussion/Council Action (5 minutes)

11

65

Document 23

The Second Meeting (Oct. 27, 2000) p. 1

The Minutes for the Judicial Council's April 28, 2000 general meeting noted on page 1 the names of the *Judicial Council members* present, including Judicial Council Chairman and California Supreme Court *Chief Justice Ronald M. George* and First District Court of Appeal Judge *Carol A. Corrigan*.

The Minutes also noted that in response to staff recommendations in the Agenda that the Judicial Council was required to revise the Firearm Restriction notice in the previous July 1, 2000 editions of the Forms DV-110 and DV-130 to conform to the notice requirements of Senate Bill 218, *each action item on the agenda was unanimously approved on the motion made and seconded.*

The Judicial Council issued this legally binding decision ten (10) months after the enactment of Senate Bill 218 on January 1, 2000.

Extract from Document 23

Judicial Council members present Chief Justice Ronald M. George; **Justices Richard D. Aldrich, Marvin R. Baxter, *Carol A. Corrigan*, and Richard D. Huffman; Judges Gail A. Andler, Aviva K. Bobb, Leonard P. Edwards, Brad R. Hill, Donna J. Hitchens, Steven E. Jahr, Ana Maria Luna, Ronald B. Robie, Ronald M. Sabraw, and Ronald L. Taylor; Mr. John J. Collins, Ms. Pauline W. Gee, and Mr. Rex A. Heeseman; and advisory members Judges William C. Harrison and Wayne L. Peterson, Commissioner Bobby R. Vincent, Mr. Fredrich Ohlrich, and Mr. Alan Slater.**

Except as noted, *each action item on the agenda was unanimously approved on the motion made and seconded.* (Tab letters and item numbers refer to the binder of Reports and Recommendations dated April 28, 2000, which was sent to members in advance of the meeting.)

JUDICIAL COUNCIL MEETING
Minutes of October 27, 2000, Meeting

The Judicial Council of California meeting began at 8:45 a.m. on Friday, October 27, 2000, at the Administrative Office of the Courts Judicial Council Conference Center in San Francisco, California, on the call of Chief Justice Ronald M. George, chair.

Judicial Council members present: Chief Justice Ronald M. George; Justices Richard D. Aldrich, Marvin R. Baxter, Carol A. Corrigan, and Richard D. Huffman; Judges Gail A. Andler, Aviva K. Bobb, Leonard P. Edwards, Brad R. Hill, Donna J. Hitchens, Steven E. Jahr, Ana Maria Luna, Ronald B. Robie, Ronald M. Sabraw, and Ronald L. Taylor; Mr. John J. Collins, Ms. Pauline W. Gee, and Mr. Rex A. Heeseman; and **advisory members:** Judges William C. Harrison and Wayne L. Peterson, Commissioner Bobby R. Vincent, Mr. Frederick K. Ohlrich, and Mr. Alan Slater.

Absent: Senator Martha Escutia; Assembly Member Darrell Steinberg; Mr. Michael Case, and Mr. Arthur Sims.

Others present included: Mr. William C. Vickrey; Hon. James A. Ardaiz, Hon. Douglas Carnahan, Hon. Mary Thornton House; Ms. Pam Aguilar, Mr. Ken Babcock, Mr. Fernando Becerra, Mr. Eric Broxmeyer, Mr. Robert W. Naylor, Mr. Tom Newton, Ms. Barbara Wheeler; **staff:** Ms. Tamara Abrams, Ms. Heather Anderson, Ms. Jessica Fiske Bailey, Mr. Michael Bergeisen, Mr. Brad Campbell, Mr. James Carroll, Mr. Blaine Corren, Ms. Penny Davis, Ms. Lesley Duncan, Ms. Diane Eisenberg, Mr. Michael Fischer, Ms. Beth Gatchalian-Litwin, Ms. Lynn Holton, Mr. Cyrus Ip, Ms. Melissa Johnson, Mr. John Larson, Mr. Ray LeBov, Mr. Dag MacLeod, Mr. Russell Mathieson, Mr. Ben McClinton, Mr. Fred Miller, Mr. Lee Morhar, Ms. Vicki Muzny, Ms. Diane Nunn, Mr. Patrick O'Donnell, Ms. Maureen O'Neil, Mr. Ronald Overholt, Wayne L. Peterson, Mr. Richard Schauffler, Ms. Anne Shelby, Ms. Dale Sipes, Ms. Lucy Smallsreed, Ms. Sonya Smith, Mr. John Sweeney, Ms. Marcia Taylor, Ms. Karen Thorson, Mr. Courtney Tucker, Ms. Alice Vilardi, Ms. Cara Vonk, Mr. Joshua Weinstein, Mr. Christopher Wu, and Ms. Pat Yerian; **media representative:** Ms. Donna Domino, *The L.A. Daily Journal;* Ms. Harriet Chiang, *San Francisco Chronicle,* Ms. Sonia Giordani, *The Recorder;* Mr. David Kravets, Associated Press, and Mr. Art Ramstein, California Service Bureau.

Except as noted, each action item on the agenda was unanimously approved on the motion made and seconded. (Tab letters and item numbers refer to the binders of Reports and Recommendations dated October 27, 2000, which were sent to members in advance of the meeting.)

Council Committee Presentations

Executive and Planning Committee
Justice Richard D. Huffman, chair, reported that the Executive and Planning Committee had met three times by phone and once in person since the last council meeting.

Document 24

The Second Decision (Oct. 27, 2000) p. 26

The Minutes of the Judicial Council's October 27, 2000 general meeting noted on page 26 that as a *Council action, Justice Huffman moved that the Judicial Council, effective January 1, 2001*, revise the Judicial Council restraining order forms *DV-110* and *DV-130 to comply with recent statutory changes.*

The Judicial Council issued this legally binding decision ten (10) months after the California Legislature enacted Senate Bill 218 on January 1, 2000.

Extract from Document 24

Council action

Justice Huffman moved that the Judicial Council, effective January 1, 2001
3. Revise Forms DV-110, Order to Show Cause and Temporary Restraining Order (CLETS)(Domestic Violence Prevention); DV-120, Responsive Declaration to Order to Show Cause (Domestic Violence Prevention); DV-130, Restraining Order After Hearing (CLETS) (Domestic Violence Prevention); DV-140, Proof of Service (Family Law---Domestic Violence Prevention--Uniform Parentage); and DV-150, Domestic Violence Restraining Orders Instruction Booklet, to comply with recent statutory changes regarding recording of prohibited communications, to reflect the name of California's new statewide child support collection entity, and to clarify issues related to proof of service and expiration date.

Declaration for Order (Domestic Violence Prevention), enabling the judicial officer to order relinquishment of firearms.

Council action:

Justice Huffman moved that the that the Judicial Council, effective January 1, 2001:

1. Revise Forms 1281, *Petition (Family Law);* 1282, *Response (Family Law);* 1296.60, *Petition to Establish Parental Relationship (Uniform Parentage);* 1296.80, *Petition for Custody and Support of Minor Children;* 1296.81, *Response to Petition for Custody and Support of Minor Children;* MC-150, *Declaration Under Uniform Child Custody Jurisdiction and Enforcement Act (UCCJEA);* and GC-210, *Petition for Appointment of Guardian of Minor,* to reflect the recent legislative adoption of the Uniform Child Custody Jurisdiction and Enforcement Act.

2. Revise Forms 1296.31B, *Child Support Information and Order Attachment (Family Law — Domestic Violence Prevention—Uniform Parentage—Governmental)* and 1296.31C, *Spousal or Family Support Order Attachment (Family Law),* to incorporate technical improvements.

3. Revise Forms DV-110, *Order to Show Cause and Temporary Restraining Order (CLETS) (Domestic Violence Prevention);* DV-120, *Responsive Declaration to Order to Show Cause (Domestic Violence Prevention);* DV-130, *Restraining Order After Hearing (CLETS) (Domestic Violence Prevention);* DV-140, *Proof of Service (Family Law—Domestic Violence Prevention—Uniform Parentage);* and DV-150, *Domestic Violence Restraining Orders Instruction Booklet,* to comply with recent statutory changes regarding recording of prohibited communications, to reflect the name of California's new statewide child support collection entity, and to clarify issues related to proof of service and expiration date.

4. Revise Form DV-100, *Application and Declaration for Order (Domestic Violence Prevention),* including the deletion of the check box opposite number 11 on the form relating to relinquishment of firearms.

The motion passed.

Item 7   **Authorizing Psychotropic Medication for Juveniles (adopt Cal. Rules of Court, rule 1432.5; adopt Form JV-220)**

Ms. Nunn, and Mr. John Sweeney, CFCC attorney, presented the item. Mr. Sweeney stated that on September 28, 1999, the Governor signed into law Senate Bill 543. The legislation requires the council to adopt rules of court, forms, and procedures to implement new and amended statutes pertaining to the administration of psychotropic medication for children who have been removed from the custody of their parents or guardians and placed under the jurisdiction of the juvenile court. The law was written to help ensure that such children receive an appropriate level of medical and mental health care. The bill does not supercede local court rules regarding the children's participation in their own mental health care planning.

70

Chapter 7
The Other Void Orders

Document 25

Form 1295.90 (Rev. Jan. 1, 2000) p. 2

The Judicial Council revised the emergency restraining order Form 1295.90 (*Emergency Protective Order*) on January 1, 2000, the same day the Legislature enacted Senate Bill 218, Penal Code Section 12021(g)(3), and Family Code Section 6389(f).

The Warnings And Information Notice on page 2 of this revision violated due process and the notice requirements of the newly amended Family Code Section 6389(f) and Penal Code Section 12021(g)(3) by failing to prohibit the restraining order respondent from *owning, possessing, purchasing, or receiving a firearm* while subject to the order.

Extract from Document 25

WARNINGS AND INFORMATION

VIOLATION OF THIS ORDER IS A MISDEMEANOR PUNISHABLE BY A $1,000 FINE, ONE YEAR IN JAIL, OR BOTH, OR MAY BE PUNISHABLE AS A FELONY. PENAL CODE SECTION 12021(G) PROHIBITS ANY PERSON SUBJECT TO A RESTRAINING ORDER FROM *PURCHASING OR ATTEMPTING TO PURCHASE OR OTHERWISE OBTAIN (sic) A FIREARM.* SUCH CONDUCT IS SUBJECT TO A $1,000 FINE AND IMPRISONMENT OR BOTH.

EMERGENCY PROTECTIVE ORDER
WARNINGS AND INFORMATION

VIOLATION OF THIS ORDER IS A MISDEMEANOR PUNISHABLE BY A $1,000 FINE, ONE YEAR IN JAIL, OR BOTH, OR MAY BE PUNISHABLE AS A FELONY. PENAL CODE SECTION 12021(g) PROHIBITS ANY PERSON SUBJECT TO A RESTRAINING ORDER FROM PURCHASING OR ATTEMPTING TO PURCHASE OR OTHERWISE OBTAIN A FIREARM. SUCH CONDUCT IS SUBJECT TO A $1,000 FINE AND IMPRISONMENT OR BOTH. THIS ORDER SHALL BE ENFORCED BY ALL LAW ENFORCEMENT OFFICERS IN THE STATE OF CALIFORNIA WHO ARE AWARE OF OR SHOWN A COPY OF THE ORDER. UNDER PENAL CODE SECTION 13710(b), "THE TERMS AND CONDITIONS OF THE PROTECTION ORDER REMAIN EN-FORCEABLE, NOTWITHSTANDING THE ACTS OF THE PARTIES, AND MAY BE CHANGED ONLY BY ORDER OF THE COURT."

To the restrained person: This order will last until the date and time in item 12 on the reverse. The protected person may, however, obtain a more permanent restraining order when the court opens. You may seek the advice of an attorney as to any matter connected with this order. The attorney should be consulted promptly so that the attorney may assist you in responding to the order.

A la persona bajo restricción judicial: Esta orden durará hasta la fecha y hora indicadas en el punto 12 al dorso. La persona protegida puede, sin embargo, obtener una Orden de entredicho (restricción judicial) más permanente cuando la corte abra. Usted puede consultar a un abogado en conexión con cualquier asunto relacionado con esta orden. Debe consultar al abogado sin pérdida de tiempo para que él o ella le pueda ayudar a responder a la orden.

To the protected person: This order will last only until the date and time noted in item 12 on the reverse. If you wish to seek continuing protection, you will have to apply for an order from the court at the address on the reverse, when it opens, or you should apply to the court in the county where you live if it is a different county and the violence is likely to occur there. You may apply for a protective order free of charge. In the case of an endangered child, you may also apply for a more permanent order at the address on the reverse, or if there is a juvenile dependency action pending you may apply for a more permanent order under section 213.5 of the Welfare and Institutions Code. In the case of a child being abducted, you may apply for a *Child Custody Order* from the court at the address on the reverse side of this form. You may seek the advice of an attorney as to any matter connected with your application for any future court orders. The attorney should be consulted promptly so that the attorney may assist you in making your application. You do not have to have an attorney to get the protective order.

A la persona protegida: Esta orden durará sólo hasta la fecha y hora indicadas en el punto 12 al dorso. Si usted desea que la protección continúe, tendrá que solicitar una orden de la corte en la dirección indicada al dorso cuando la corte abra, o tendrá que hacer la solicitud ante la corte del condado donde usted vive, si se trata de un condado diferente y es probable que la violencia ocurra allí. La solicitud de la orden de protección es gratis. En el caso de que un niño o una niña se encuentre en peligro, puede solicitar una orden más permanente en la dirección indicada al dorso o, si hay una acción legal pendiente de tutela juvenil, puede solicitar una orden más permanente conforme a la sección 213.5 del código titulado en inglés **Welfare and Institutions Code.** En el caso del secuestro de un niño o una niña, usted puede solicitar de la corte una Orden para la guarda del niño o de la niña *(Child Custody Order),* en la dirección indicada al dorso de este formulario. Puede consultar a un abogado en conexión con cualquier asunto relacionado con las solicitudes de órdenes de la corte que usted presente en el futuro. Debe consultar un abogado sin perdida de tiempo para que él o ella le pueda ayudar a presentar su solicitud. Para obtener la orden de protección no es necesario que un abogado le represente.

To law enforcement: Penal Code section 13710(c) provides that, upon request, law enforcement shall serve the party to be restrained at the scene of a domestic violence incident or at any time the restrained party is in custody. The officer who requested the emergency protective order, while on duty, shall carry copies of the order. The emergency protective order shall be served upon the restrained party by the officer, if the restrained party can reasonably be located, and a copy shall be given to the protected party. A copy also shall be filed with the court as soon as practicable after issuance. The availability of an emergency protective order shall not be affected by the fact that the endangered person has vacated the household to avoid abuse. A law enforcement officer shall use every reasonable means to enforce an emergency protective order issued pursuant to this subdivision. A law enforcement officer acting pursuant to this subdivision shall not be held civilly or criminally liable if he or she has acted in good faith with regard thereto.

If a child is in danger of being abducted: This order will last only until the date and time noted in the *Emergency Protective Order.* You may apply for a child custody order from the court, on the reverse side of this form.

En el caso de peligro de secuestro de un niño o de una niña: Esta orden será válida sólo hasta la hora y fecha indicadas en la Orden de protección de emergencia *(Emergency Protective Order).* Usted puede solicitar de la corte una Orden para la guarda del niño o de la niña *(Child Custody Order),* en la dirección indicada al dorso.

This emergency protective order is effective when made. This order shall expire not later than the close of judicial business on the fifth day of judicial business following the day of its issue. An emergency protective order is also available to prevent the occurrence of child abuse.

1295.90 [Rev. January 1, 2000]

EMERGENCY PROTECTIVE ORDER (CLETS)
(Domestic Violence, Child Abuse, Elder or Dependent
Adult Abuse, Workplace Violence, Civil Harassment)

Page two

ONE copy to court, ONE copy to restrained person, ONE copy to protected person, ONE copy to issuing agency

Document 26

Form EPO-001 (Rev. Jan. 1, 2004) p. 2

The Judicial Council revised the emergency restraining order Form EPO-001 (*Emergency Protective Order*) again on January 1, 2004, four (4) years after the enactment of S.B. 218, Penal Code Section 12021(g)(3), and Family Code Section 6389(f) on January 1, 2000.

The Warnings And Information notice on page 2 of this revision conformed to the notice requirements of amended Family Code Section 6389(f) and Penal Code Section 12021(g)(3) by prohibiting the restraining order respondent from *owning, possessing, purchasing, receiving, or attempting to purchase or receive a firearm.*

Extract from Document 26

WARNINGS AND INFORMATION

VIOLATION OF THIS ORDER IS A MISDEMEANOR PUNISHABLE BY A $1,000 FINE, ONE YEAR IN JAIL, OR BOTH, OR MAY BE PUNISHABLE AS A FELONY. PERSONS SUBJECT TO A RESTRAINING ORDER ARE PROHIBITED F R O M *OWNING, POSSESSING, PURCHASING, RECEIVING, OR ATTEMPTING TO PURCHASE OR RECEIVE A FIREARM* (PENAL CODE SECTION 12021(g). SUCH CONDUCT IS SUBJECT TO A $1,000 FINE AND IMPRISONMENT OR BOTH.

EMERGENCY PROTECTIVE ORDER
WARNINGS AND INFORMATION

VIOLATION OF THIS ORDER IS A MISDEMEANOR PUNISHABLE BY A $1,000 FINE, ONE YEAR IN JAIL, OR BOTH, OR MAY BE PUNISHABLE AS A FELONY. PERSONS SUBJECT TO A RESTRAINING ORDER ARE PROHIBITED FROM OWNING, POSSESSING, PURCHASING, RECEIVING, OR ATTEMPTING TO PURCHASE OR RECEIVE A FIREARM (PENAL CODE SECTION 12021(g)). SUCH CONDUCT IS SUBJECT TO A $1,000 FINE AND IMPRISONMENT OR BOTH. THIS ORDER SHALL BE ENFORCED BY ALL LAW ENFORCEMENT OFFICERS IN THE STATE OF CALIFORNIA WHO ARE AWARE OF OR SHOWN A COPY OF THE ORDER. UNDER PENAL CODE SECTION 13710(b), "THE TERMS AND CONDITIONS OF THE PROTECTION ORDER REMAIN ENFORCEABLE, NOTWITHSTANDING THE ACTS OF THE PARTIES, AND MAY BE CHANGED ONLY BY ORDER OF THE COURT."

To the restrained person: This order will last until the date and time in item 12 on the reverse. The protected person may, however, obtain a more permanent restraining order from the court. You may seek the advice of an attorney as to any matter connected with this order. The attorney should be consulted promptly so that the attorney may assist you in responding to the order.

A la persona bajo restricción judicial: Esta orden durará hasta la fecha y hora indicadas en el punto 12 al dorso. La persona protegida puede, sin embargo, obtener una Orden de entredicho (restricción judicial) más permanente de la corte. Usted puede consultar a un abogado en conexión con cualquier asunto relacionado con esta orden. Debe consultar al abogado sin pérdida de tiempo para que él o ella le pueda ayudar a responder a la orden.

To the protected person: This order will last only until the date and time noted in item 12 on the reverse. If you wish to seek continuing protection, you will have to apply for an order from the court at the address in item 13, or you should apply to the court in the county where you live if it is a different county and the violence is likely to occur there. You may apply for a protective order free of charge. In the case of an endangered child, you may also apply for a more permanent order at the address in item 13, or if there is a juvenile dependency action pending you may apply for a more permanent order under section 213.5 of the Welfare and Institutions Code. In the case of a child being abducted, you may apply for a *Child Custody Order* from the court at the address in item 13. You may seek the advice of an attorney as to any matter connected with your application for any future court orders. The attorney should be consulted promptly so that the attorney may assist you in making your application. You do not have to have an attorney to get the protective order.

A la persona protegida: Esta orden durará sólo hasta la fecha y hora indicadas en el punto 12 al dorso. Si usted desea que la protección continúe, tendrá que solicitar una orden de la corte en la dirección indicada en el articulo 13, o tendrá que hacer la solicitud ante la corte del condado donde usted vive, si se trata de un condado diferente y es probable que la violencia ocurra allí. La solicitud de la orden de protección es gratis. En el caso de que un niño o una niña se encuentre en peligro, puede solicitar una orden más permanente en la dirección indicada en el articulo 13 o, si hay una acción legal pendiente de tutela juvenil, puede solicitar una orden más permanente conforme a la sección 213.5 del código titulado en inglés **Welfare and Institutions Code.** En el caso del secuestro de un niño o una niña, usted puede solicitar de la corte una Orden para la guarda del niño o de la niña *(Child Custody Order)*, en la dirección indicada en el articulo 13 de este formulario. Puede consultar a un abogado en conexión con cualquier asunto relacionado con las solicitudes de órdenes de la corte que usted presente en el futuro. Debe consultar un abogado sin perdida de tiempo para que él o ella le pueda ayudar a presentar su solicitud. Para obtener la orden de protección no es necesario que un abogado le represente.

To law enforcement: Penal Code section 13710(c) provides that, upon request, law enforcement shall serve the party to be restrained at the scene of a domestic violence incident or at any time the restrained party is in custody. The officer who requested the emergency protective order, while on duty, shall carry copies of the order. The emergency protective order shall be served upon the restrained party by the officer, if the restrained party can reasonably be located, and a copy shall be given to the protected party. A copy also shall be filed with the court as soon as practicable after issuance. The availability of an emergency protective order shall not be affected by the fact that the endangered person has vacated the household to avoid abuse. A law enforcement officer shall use every reasonable means to enforce an emergency protective order issued pursuant to this subdivision. A law enforcement officer acting pursuant to this subdivision shall not be held civilly or criminally liable if he or she has acted in good faith with regard thereto.

If a child is in danger of being abducted: This order will last only until the date and time noted in item 12 on the reverse. You may apply for a child custody order from the court.

En el caso de peligro de secuestro de un niño o de una niña: Esta orden será válida sólo hasta la hora y fecha indicadas en el punto 12 al dorso. Usted puede solicitar de la corte una Orden para la guarda del niño o de la niña *(Child Custody Order).*

This emergency protective order is effective when made. This order shall expire not later than the close of judicial business on the fifth day of judicial business or the seventh calendar day following the day of its issue. A protective order issued in a criminal case on form CR-160 or MC-220 takes precedence in enforcement over any conflicting civil court order.

EPO-001 [Rev. January 1, 2004]

EMERGENCY PROTECTIVE ORDER (CLETS)
(Domestic Violence, Child Abuse, Elder or Dependent
Adult Abuse, or Stalking (Workplace Violence, Civil Harassment))
ONE copy to court, ONE copy to restrained person, ONE copy to protected person, ONE copy to issuing agency

Page two

Document 27

Form CH-120 (Rev. Jan. 1, 1999) p. 2

The Judicial Council republished the revised January 1, 1999 civil harassment temporary restraining order Form CH-120 (*Order to Show Cause and Temporary Restraining Order*) on January 1, 2000, the same day the Legislature enacted Senate Bill 218, Penal Code Section 12021(g)(3), and Family Code Section 6389(f).

The violations notice on page 2 of this revision violated due process and the notice requirements of the newly amended Family Code Section 6389(f) and Penal Code Section 12021(g)(3) by failing to prohibit the restraining order respondent from *owning, possessing, purchasing, or receiving a firearm* while subjected to the protective order.

Extract from Document 27

By California state law, violation of this temporary restraining order is a misdemeanor, punishable by one year in jail, a $1,000 fine, or both, or may be punishable as a felony. Any person subject to a restraining order is prohibited from *purchasing or attempting to purchase, receiving or attempting to receive, or otherwise obtaining a firearm*. Such conduct is subject to a $1,000 fine and imprisonment. If a final order is entered against the restrained person after the hearing, even if the restrained person did not attend, he or she may be prohibited from possessing, transporting, or accepting a firearm under the 1994 amendments to the Gun Control Act, 18 U.S.C. § 922(g)(8). A violation of this prohibition is a separate offense.

PLAINTIFF (Name):	CASE NUMBER:
DEFENDANT (Name):	

6. ☐ OTHER ORDERS (specify):

7. By the close of business on the date of this order, a copy of this order and any proof of service shall be given to the law enforcement agencies listed below as follows:
   a. ☐ plaintiff shall deliver.
   b. ☐ plaintiff's attorney shall deliver.
   c. ☐ the clerk of the court shall deliver.

   Law enforcement agency   Address

8. a. ☐ Application for an order shortening time is granted and the following documents shall be personally served on the defendant no fewer than (specify number): _____ days before the time set for hearing.
   b. ☐ The following documents shall be personally served on defendant within five days from the date the TRO is issued, or two days before the hearing, whichever is earlier:
      (1) Order to Show Cause (Harassment) and Temporary Restraining Order
      (2) Petition for Injunction Prohibiting Harassment (form CH-100)
      (3) Blank Response to Petition for Injunction Prohibiting Harassment (form CH-110)
      (4) Other (specify):

9. ☐ Filing fees for the filing of this action are duly waived.

Date: _____

_____
JUDICIAL OFFICER

This order is effective when made. It is enforceable in all 50 states, the District of Columbia, all tribal lands, and all U.S. territories, and shall be enforced as if it were an order of that jurisdiction by any law enforcement agency that has received the order, is shown a copy of the order, or has verified its existence on the California Law Enforcement Telecommunications System (CLETS). If proof of service on the restrained person has not been received, and the restrained person was not present at the court hearing, the law enforcement agency shall advise the restrained person of the terms of the order and then shall enforce it. Violations of this restraining order are subject to federal and state criminal penalties. By California state law, violation of this temporary restraining order is a misdemeanor, punishable by one year in jail, a $1,000 fine, or both, or may be punishable as a felony. Any person subject to a restraining order is prohibited from purchasing or attempting to purchase, receiving or attempting to receive, or otherwise obtaining a firearm. Such conduct is subject to a $1,000 fine and imprisonment. If a final order is entered against the restrained person after the hearing, even if the restrained person did not attend, he or she may be prohibited from possessing, transporting, or accepting a firearm under the 1994 amendments to the Gun Control Act, 18 U.S.C. § 922(g)(8). A violation of this prohibition is a separate offense.

[SEAL]	**CLERK'S CERTIFICATE** I certify that the foregoing Order to Show Cause and Temporary Restraining Order (CLETS) is a true and correct copy of the original on file in the court.
	Date: _____ Clerk, by _____ , Deputy

CH-120 [Rev. January 1, 1999]

ORDER TO SHOW CAUSE AND
TEMPORARY RESTRAINING ORDER (CLETS)
(Harassment)

Page two

Document 28
Form CH-120 (Rev. July 1, 2000) p. 2

The Judicial Council revised the civil harassment temporary restraining order Form CH-120 (*Order to Show Cause and Temporary Restraining Order*) on July 1, 2000, six (6) months after the enactment of Senate Bill 218, Penal Code Section 12021(g)(3), and Family Code Section 6389(f) on January 1, 2000.

The violations notice on page 2 of this revision violated due process and the notice requirements of the newly amended Family Code Section 6389(f) and Penal Code Section 12021(g)(3) by failing to prohibit the restraining order respondent from *owning, possessing, purchasing, or receiving a firearm* while subjected to the protective order.

Extract from Document 28

By California state law, violation of this temporary retraining order is a misdemeanor, punishable by one year in jail, a $1,000 fine, or both, or may be punishable as a felony. Any person subject to a restraining order is prohibited from *purchasing or attempting to purchase, receiving or attempting to receive, or otherwise obtaining a firearm*. Such conduct is subject to a $1,000 fine and imprisonment.

PLAINTIFF (Name):	CASE NUMBER:
DEFENDANT (Name):	

6. ☐ OTHER ORDERS (specify):

7. By the close of business on the date of this order, a copy of this order and any proof of service shall be given to the law enforcement agencies listed below as follows:
   a. ☐ plaintiff shall deliver.
   b. ☐ plaintiff's attorney shall deliver.
   c. ☐ the clerk of the court shall deliver.

   Law enforcement agency   Address

8. a. ☐ Application for an order shortening time is granted and the following documents shall be personally served on the defendant no fewer than (specify number): _____ days before the time set for hearing.
   b. ☐ The following documents shall be personally served on defendant within five days from the date the TRO is issued, or two days before the hearing, whichever is earlier:
      (1) Order to Show Cause (Harassment) and Temporary Restraining Order
      (2) Petition for Injunction Prohibiting Harassment (form CH-100)
      (3) Blank Response to Petition for Injunction Prohibiting Harassment (form CH-110)
      (4) Other (specify):

9. ☐ Filing fees for the filing of this action are duly waived.

Date: _____

_____
JUDICIAL OFFICER

This order is effective when made. It is enforceable in all 50 states, the District of Columbia, all tribal lands, and all U.S. territories, and shall be enforced as if it were an order of that jurisdiction by any law enforcement agency that has received the order, is shown a copy of the order, or has verified its existence on the California Law Enforcement Telecommunications System (CLETS). If proof of service on the restrained person has not been received, and the restrained person was not present at the court hearing, the law enforcement agency shall advise the restrained person of the terms of the order and then shall enforce it. Violations of this restraining order are subject to federal and state criminal penalties. By California state law, violation of this temporary restraining order is a misdemeanor, punishable by one year in jail, a $1,000 fine, or both, or may be punishable as a felony. Any person subject to a restraining order is prohibited from purchasing or attempting to purchase, receiving or attempting to receive, or otherwise obtaining a firearm. Such conduct is subject to a $1,000 fine and imprisonment. If a final order is entered against the restrained person after the hearing, even if the restrained person did not attend, he or she may be prohibited from possessing, transporting, or accepting a firearm under the 1994 amendments to the Gun Control Act, 18 U.S.C. § 922(g)(8). A violation of this prohibition is a separate offense.

[SEAL]	**CLERK'S CERTIFICATE**
	I certify that the foregoing Order to Show Cause and Temporary Restraining Order (CLETS) is a true and correct copy of the original on file in the court.
	Date: _____ Clerk, by _____, Deputy

CH-120 [Rev. July 1, 2000]

**ORDER TO SHOW CAUSE AND
TEMPORARY RESTRAINING ORDER (CLETS)
(Harassment)**

Page two

Document 29

Form CH-120 (Rev. Jan. 1, 2003) p. 3

The Judicial Council revised the civil harassment temporary restraining order Form CH-120 (*Order to Show Cause and Temporary Restraining Order*) on January 1, 2003, three (3) years after the enactment of Senate Bill 218, Penal Code Section 12021(g)(3), and Family Code Section 6389(f) on January 1, 2000.

The Notice Regarding Firearms on page 3 of this revision conformed to the notice requirements of amended Family Code Section 6389(f) and Penal Code Section 12021(g)(3) by prohibiting the respondent from *owning, possessing, purchasing or attempting to purchase, receiving or attempting to receive, or otherwise obtaining a firearm.*

Extract from Document 29

NOTICE REGARDING FIREARMS

Any person subject to a restraining order is prohibited from *owning, possessing, purchasing or attempting to purchase, receiving or attempting to receive, or otherwise obtaining a firearm.* Such conduct is subject to a $1,000 fine and imprisonment.

<table>
<tr><td>PLAINTIFF (Name):</td><td rowspan="2">CASE NUMBER:</td></tr>
<tr><td>DEFENDANT (Name):</td></tr>
</table>

9. a. ☐ Application for an order shortening time is granted and the documents listed in b shall be personally served on the defendant no fewer than (specify number): _____ days before the time set for hearing.

   b. ☐ The following documents shall be personally served on defendant:

     (1) Order to Show Cause and Temporary Restraining Order (Harassment) (form CH-120)

     (2) Petition for Injunction Prohibiting Harassment (form CH-100)

     (3) Blank Response to Petition for Injunction Prohibiting Harassment (form CH-110)

     (4) Instructions for Lawsuits to Prohibit Harassment (form CH-150)

     (5) Other (specify):

10. ☐ Filing fees for the filing of this action are duly waived.

Date: _____

_____
JUDICIAL OFFICER

This order is effective when made. It is enforceable anywhere in all 50 states, the District of Columbia, all tribal lands, and all U.S. territories and shall be enforced as if it were an order of that jurisdiction by any law enforcement agency that has received the order, is shown a copy of the order, or has verified its existence on the California Law Enforcement Telecommunications System (CLETS). If proof of service on the restrained person has not been received, and the restrained person was not present at the court hearing, the law enforcement agency shall advise the restrained person of the terms of the order and then shall enforce it. Violations of this restraining order are subject to criminal penalties.

NOTICE REGARDING FIREARMS

Any person subject to a restraining order is prohibited from owning, possessing, purchasing or attempting to purchase, receiving or attempting to receive, or otherwise obtaining a firearm. Such conduct is subject to a $1,000 fine and imprisonment.

[SEAL]

CLERK'S CERTIFICATE

I certify that the foregoing Order to Show Cause and Temporary Restraining Order (CLETS) is a true and correct copy of the original on file in the court.

Date: _____   Clerk, by _____, Deputy

CH-120 [Rev. January 1, 2003]

ORDER TO SHOW CAUSE AND
TEMPORARY RESTRAINING ORDER (CLETS)
(Harassment)

Page 3 of 3

Document 30

Form CH-140 (Rev. Jan. 1, 1999), p. 2

The Judicial Council republished the revised January 1, 1999 edition of the civil harassment restraining order Form CH-140 (*Order After Hearing on Petition for Injunction Prohibiting Harassment*) on January 1, 2000, the same day the Legislature enacted Senate Bill 218, Penal Code Section 12021(g)(3), and Family Code Section 6389(f).

The violations notice on page 2 of this republished revision violated due process and the notice requirement of the newly amended Family Code Section 6389(f) and Penal Code Section 12021(g)(3) by failing to prohibit the restraining order respondent from *owning, possessing, purchasing, or receiving a firearm* while subjected to the protective order.

Extract from Document 30

By California state law, violation of this temporary restraining order is a misdemeanor, punishable by one year in jail, a $1,000 fine, or both, or may be punishable as a felony. Any person subject to a restraining order is *prohibited from purchasing or attempting to purchase, receiving or attempting to receive, or otherwise obtaining a firearm*. Such conduct is subject to a $1,000 fine and imprisonment.

PLAINTIFF *(Name)*:	CASE NUMBER:
DEFENDANT *(Name)*:	

7. ☐ Other orders *(specify)*:

8. By the close of business on the date of this order, a copy of this order and any proof of service shall be given to the law enforcement agencies listed below as follows:
   a. ☐ plaintiff shall deliver.
   b. ☐ plaintiff's attorney shall deliver.
   c. ☐ the clerk of the court shall deliver.
            Law enforcement agency   Address

Date:

_____
JUDICIAL OFFICER'S SIGNATURE

CERTIFICATION OF COMPLIANCE WITH VAWA This order meets all Full Faith and Credit requirements of the Violence Against Women Act, 18 U.S.C. § 2265 (1994) (VAWA). This court has jurisdiction over the parties and the subject matter; the defendant has been afforded notice and a timely opportunity to be heard as provided by the laws of this jurisdiction. This order is valid and entitled to enforcement in this and all other jurisdictions.

This order is effective when made. It is enforceable in all 50 states, the District of Columbia, all tribal lands, and all U.S. territories, and shall be enforced as if it were an order of that jurisdiction by any law enforcement agency that has received the order, is shown a copy of the order, or has verified its existence on the California Law Enforcement Telecommunications System (CLETS). If proof of service on the restrained person has not been received, and the restrained person was not present at the court hearing, the law enforcement agency shall advise the restrained person of the terms of the order and then shall enforce it. Violations of this restraining order are subject to federal and state criminal penalties. By California state law, violation of this temporary restraining order is a misdemeanor, punishable by one year in jail, a $1,000 fine, or both, or may be punishable as a felony. Any person subject to a restraining order is prohibited from purchasing or attempting to purchase, receiving or attempting to receive, or otherwise obtaining a firearm. Such conduct is subject to a $1,000 fine and imprisonment.

[SEAL]	**CLERK'S CERTIFICATE**
	I certify that the foregoing *Order After Hearing on Petition for Injunction Prohibiting Harassment (CLETS)* is a true and correct copy of the original on file in the court.
	Date: Clerk, by _____ , Deputy

CH-140 [Rev. January 1, 1999]

ORDER AFTER HEARING ON PETITION FOR INJUNCTION PROHIBITING HARASSMENT (CLETS)

Page two

Document 31

Form CH-140 (Rev. Jan. 1, 2003) p. 2

The Judicial Council revised the civil harassment restraining order Form CH-140 (*Order After Hearing on Petition for Injunction Prohibiting Harassment*) on January 1, 2003, three (3) years after the enactment of Senate Bill 218, Penal Code Section 12021(g)(3), and Family Code Sections 6389(c) and 6389(f) on January 1, 2000.

The Mandatory Firearm Relinquishment notice on page 2 of this revision conformed to the notice requirements of amended Family Code Section 6389(c) by referring to the presence or the absence of the restraining order respondent at a prior noticed court hearing with two parenthetical phrases: *If restrained person is present at hearing* and *If restrained person is not present at hearing*.

The Notice Regarding Firearms in this revision conformed to the notice requirements of amended Family Code Section 6389(f) and Penal Code Section 12021(g)(3) by prohibiting the respondent from *owning, possessing, purchasing or attempting to purchase, receiving or attempting to receive, or otherwise obtaining a firearm.*

Extract from Document 31

8. MANDATORY FIREARM RELINQUISHMENT

The restrained person must surrender to local law enforcement or sell to a licensed gun dealer any firearm in or subject to his or her immediate possession or control within

a. 24 hours after issuance of this order (*If restrained person is present at hearing*).
b. 48 hours after service of this order (*If restrained person is not present at hearing*).
c. other (specify)

NOTICE REGARDING FIREARMS

Any person subject to a restraining order is prohibited from *owning, possessing, purchasing or attempting to purchase, receiving or attempting to receive, or otherwise obtaining a firearm.* Such conduct is subject to a $1,000 fine and imprisonment.

PLAINTIFF (Name):	CASE NUMBER:
DEFENDANT (Name):	

6. b. ☐ **shall** stay at least *(specify)*: _____ **yards** away from the following protected persons and places:

    (1) ☐ Person seeking the order

    (2) ☐ The other protected persons listed in item 5c

    (3) ☐ Residence of person seeking the order

    (4) ☐ Place of work of person seeking the order

    (5) ☐ The children's school or place of child care

    (6) ☐ The protected persons' vehicles

    (7) ☐ Other *(specify)*:

7. ☐ Other orders *(specify)*:

8. **MANDATORY FIREARM RELINQUISHMENT**

The restrained person must surrender to local law enforcement or sell to a licensed gun dealer any firearm in or subject to his or her immediate possession or control within

    a. ☐ 24 hours after issuance of this order (if restrained person is present at hearing).

    b. ☐ 24 hours after service of this order (if restrained person is not present at hearing).

    c. ☐ other *(specify)*:

The restrained person shall file a receipt with the court showing compliance with this order within 72 hours of receiving this order.

9. By the close of business on the date of this order, a copy of this order and any proof of service shall be given to the law enforcement agencies listed below as follows:

    a. ☐ plaintiff shall deliver.

    b. ☐ plaintiff's attorney shall deliver.

    c. ☐ the clerk of the court shall deliver.

        Law enforcement agency   Address

Date: _____

_____
JUDICIAL OFFICER'S SIGNATURE

This order is effective when made. It is enforceable anywhere in all 50 states, the District of Columbia, all tribal lands, and all U.S. territories and shall be enforced as if it were an order of that jurisdiction by any law enforcement agency that has received the order, is shown a copy of the order, or has verified its existence on the California Law Enforcement Telecommunications System (CLETS). If proof of service on the restrained person has not been received, and the restrained person was not present at the court hearing, the law enforcement agency shall advise the restrained person of the terms of the order and then shall enforce it. Violations of this restraining order are subject to criminal penalties.

NOTICE REGARDING FIREARMS

Any person subject to a restraining order is prohibited from owning, possessing, purchasing or attempting to purchase, receiving or attempting to receive, or otherwise obtaining a firearm. Such conduct is subject to a $1,000 fine and imprisonment.

[SEAL]	**CLERK'S CERTIFICATE**
	I certify that the foregoing *Order After Hearing on Petition for Injunction Prohibiting Harassment (CLETS)* is a true and correct copy of the original on file in the court.
	Date: _____ Clerk, by _____ , Deputy

ORDER AFTER HEARING ON PETITION FOR INJUNCTION PROHIBITING HARASSMENT (CLETS)

Document 32

Form EA-120 (New April 1, 2000) p. 3

The Judicial Council published a new elder abuse temporary restraining order Form EA-120 (*Order to Show Cause and Temporary Restraining Order*) on April 1, 2000, three (3) months after the enactment of Senate Bill 218, Penal Code Section 12021(g)(3), and Family Code Section 6389(f) on January 1, 2000.

The Notice Regarding Enforcement Of This Order on page 3 of this new form violated due process and the notice requirements of the newly amended Family Code Section 6389(f) and Penal Code Section 12021(g)(3) by failing to prohibit the restraining order respondent from *owning, possessing, purchasing, or receiving a firearm.*

Extract from Document 32

NOTICE REGARDING ENFORCEMENT OF THIS ORDER

Violation of this restraining order may be punishable as a contempt of court, a misdemeanor, punishable by one year in jail or a $1,000 fine, or both, *or a felony.*

PETITIONER:	CASE NUMBER:
RESPONDENT:	

11. *(Continued)*

Law enforcement agency   Address

Date: _____   _____
                                                                            JUDICIAL OFFICER

NOTICES TO THE RESPONDENT

WHAT FORMS YOU SHOULD FILE IN RESPONSE AND WHEN TO FILE THEM

An original *Response to Petition for Protective Orders* (form EA-110) must be filed with the court and a copy served on the petitioner or the petitioner's attorney at least two court days before the hearing date unless the judge has shortened time for service (see item 10 in this *Order to Show Cause and Temporary Restraining Order*). You do not have to pay any fee to file your response. Before completing your response, you should read the *Instructions for the Respondent* on the next page.

NOTICE REGARDING FAILURE TO APPEAR AT HEARING

If you have been personally served with a temporary restraining order, but you do not appear at the hearing either in person or by counsel, and a restraining order is issued at the hearing which does not differ from the prior temporary restraining order, a copy of the order will be served upon you by mail at the following address:

If that address is not correct or you wish to verify that the temporary order was made permanent without substantive change, you should contact the clerk of the court.

NOTICE REGARDING ENFORCEMENT OF THIS ORDER

This order is effective when made. It is enforceable anywhere in California by any law enforcement agency that has received the order, is shown a copy of the order, or has verified its existence on the California Law Enforcement Telecommunications System (CLETS). If proof of service on the restrained person has not been received, and the restrained person was not present at the court hearing, the law enforcement agency shall advise the restrained person of the terms of the order and shall enforce it.

Violation of this restraining order may be punished as a contempt of court, a misdemeanor, punishable by one year in jail or a $1,000 fine, or both, or a felony.

[SEAL]	CLERK'S CERTIFICATE
	I certify that the foregoing *Order to Show Cause and Temporary Restraining Order (Elder or Dependent Adult Abuse) (CLETS)* is a true and correct copy of the original on file in the court. Date: _____ Clerk, by _____ , Deputy

(Continued on reverse)

EA-120 [New April 1, 2000]

**ORDER TO SHOW CAUSE
AND TEMPORARY RESTRAINING ORDER
(Elder or Dependent Adult Abuse) (CLETS)**

Page three of four

Document 33

Form EA-120 (Rev. Jan. 1, 2001) p. 3

The Judicial Council revised the elder abuse temporary restraining order Form EA-120 (*Order to Show Cause and Temporary Restraining Order*) on January 1, 2001, one (1) year after the enactment of Senate Bill 218, Penal Code Section 12021(g)(3), and Family Code Section 6389(f) on January 1, 2000.

The Notice Regarding Enforcement Of This Order on page 3 of this revision violated due process and the notice requirements of amended Family Code Section 6389(f) and Penal Code Section 12021(g)(3) by failing to prohibit the restraining order respondent from *owning, possessing, purchasing, or receiving a firearm* while subjected to the order.

Extract from Document 33

NOTICE REGARDING ENFORCEMENT OF THIS ORDER

Violation of this order *may be punishable as a contempt of court, a misdemeanor*, punishable by one year in jail or a $1,000 fine, or both, or a felony.

PETITIONER:			NUMBER:
RESPONDENT:			

10. *(Continued)*

        Law enforcement agency   Address

Date: _____

                                                                    _____

                                                                     JUDICIAL OFFICER

NOTICES TO THE RESPONDENT

IMPORTANT INFORMATION FOR RESTRAINED PERSON

Carefully read these and all other papers served on you. The *Order to Show Cause and Temporary Restraining Order (Elder or Dependent Adult Abuse)* [OSC] tells you when to appear in court and may contain a temporary restraining order forbidding you from doing certain things. If you disobey the court's orders, criminal charges may be filed against you.

If you want to respond to or oppose the *Petition for Protective Orders (Elder or Dependent Adult Abuse)* [Petition], you should file a *Response to Petition for Protective Orders* [Response] (Form EA-110). Read the *Instructions for the Respondent* on the next page for information on how to complete your Response.

NOTICE REGARDING ENFORCEMENT OF THIS ORDER

This order is effective when made. It is enforceable anywhere in California by any law enforcement agency that has received the order, is shown a copy of the order, or has verified its existence on the California Law Enforcement Telecommunications System (CLETS). If proof of service on the restrained person has not been received, and the restrained person was not present at the court hearing, the law enforcement agency shall advise the restrained person of the terms of the order and shall enforce it.

Violation of this restraining order may be punished as a contempt of court, a misdemeanor, punishable by one year in jail or a $1,000 fine, or both.

[SEAL]

CLERK'S CERTIFICATE

I certify that the foregoing *Order to Show Cause and Temporary Restraining Order (Elder or Dependent Adult Abuse) (CLETS)* is a true and correct copy of the original on file in the court.

Date: _____   Clerk, by _____, Deputy

(Continued on reverse)

EA-120 [Rev. January 1, 2001]   **ORDER TO SHOW CAUSE AND TEMPORARY RESTRAINING ORDER (Elder or Dependent Adult Abuse) (CLETS)**   Page three of four

89

Document 34

Form EA-120 (Rev. July 1, 2004) p. 3

The Judicial Council revised the elder abuse temporary restraining order Form EA-120 (*Order to Show Cause and Temporary Restraining Order*) again on January 1, 2004, four (4) years after the California Legislature enacted Senate Bill 218, Penal Code Section 12021(g)(3), and Family Code Section 6389(f) on January 1, 2000.

The Notice Regarding Firearms on page 3 of this revision conformed to the notice requirements of amended Family Code Section 6389(f) and Penal Code Section 12021(g)(3) by prohibiting the respondent from *owning, possessing, purchasing, or receiving, or attempting to purchase or receive, a firearm* while subjected to the protective order.

Extract from Document 34

NOTICE REGARDING FIREARMS

Unless this case involves solely financial abuse unaccompanied by force, threat, harassment, intimidation, or other form of abuse, any person subject to a restraining order is *prohibited from owning, possessing, purchasing, or receiving, or attempting to purchase or receive, a firearm*. Such conduct is subject to a $1,000 fine and imprisonment.

c. The documents listed below must be personally served on the restrained person:

1. ☐ *Petition for Protective Orders (Elder or Dependent Adult Abuse) (CLETS).*
2. ☐ *Order to Show Cause and Temporary Restraining Order (Elder or Dependent Adult Abuse) (CLETS).*
3. ☐ Blank *Response Petition for Protective Orders (Elder or Dependent Adult Abuse) (CLETS).*
4. ☐ Other *(specify):*

d. Proof of service of the documents must be served and filed with the court before the hearing.

11. **DELIVERY TO LAW ENFORCEMENT**

A copy of this order and any proof of service must be delivered to the law enforcement agencies listed below by the following means:

a. ☐ The protected person must deliver.
b. ☐ The protected person's attorney must deliver.
c. ☐ The clerk of the court must mail.

Law enforcement agency   Address

Date: _____   _____
                                                   JUDICIAL OFFICER

NOTICES TO THE RESPONDENT

IMPORTANT INFORMATION FOR RESTRAINED PERSON

Carefully read these and all other papers served on you. The *Order to Show Cause and Temporary Restraining Order (Elder or Dependent Adult Abuse)* **[OSC] tells you when to appear in court and may contain a temporary restraining order forbidding you from doing certain things. If you disobey the court's orders, criminal charges may be filed against you.**

If you want to respond to or oppose the *Petition for Protective Orders (Elder or Dependent Adult Abuse)* [Petition], you should file a *Response to Petition for Protective Orders* [Response] (Form EA-110). Read the *Instructions for the Respondent* on the next page for information on how to complete your Response.

NOTICE REGARDING ENFORCEMENT OF THIS ORDER

This order is effective when made. It is enforceable anywhere in California by any law enforcement agency that has received the order, is shown a copy of the order, or has verified its existence on the California Law Enforcement Telecommunications System (CLETS). If proof of service on the restrained person has not been received, and the restrained person was not present at the court hearing, the law enforcement agency shall advise the restrained person of the terms of the order and shall enforce it.

Violation of this restraining order may be punished as a contempt of court, a misdemeanor, punishable by one year in jail or a $1,000 fine, or both.

NOTICE REGARDING FIREARMS

Unless this case involves solely financial abuse unaccompanied by force, threat, harassment, intimidation, or other form of abuse, any person subject to a restraining order is prohibited from owning, possessing, purchasing, or receiving, or attempting to purchase or receive, a firearm. Such conduct is subject to a $1,000 fine and imprisonment.

EA-120 [Rev. July 1, 2004]

**ORDER TO SHOW CAUSE
AND TEMPORARY RESTRAINING ORDER
(Elder or Dependent Adult Abuse) (CLETS)**

Page 3 of 4

Document 35

Form EA-130 (New April 1, 2000) p. 2

The Judicial Council published a new elder abuse post-hearing restraining order Form EA-120 (*Restraining Order After Hearing*) on April 1, 2000, three (3) months after the California Legislature enacted Senate Bill 218, Penal Code Section 12021(g)(3), and Family Code Section 6389(f) on January 1, 2000.

The violations notice on page 2 of this new form violated due process and the notice requirements of the newly amended Family Code Section 6389(f) and Penal Code Section 12021(g)(3) by failing to prohibit the restraining order respondent from *owning, possessing, purchasing, or receiving a firearm* while subjected to the protective order.

Extract from Document 35

Violation of this order is a misdemeanor, punishable by a $1,000 fine, one year in jail, or both, or may be punishable as a felony. This order shall be enforced by all law enforcement officers in the State of California. Any person subject to a restraining order is *prohibited from obtaining or attempting to obtain or purchase a firearm* by Penal Code section 12021. Such conduct may be a felony and punishable by a $1,000 fine and imprisonment.

PETITIONER:	CASE NUMBER:
RESPONDENT:	

7. ☐ **RESIDENCE EXCLUSION ORDER**

The restrained person **must** immediately move from the residence located at the address stated in item 5 above.

8. ☐ **STAY-AWAY ORDER**

The restrained person **must** stay at least (specify): _____ **yards** away from the following persons and places:

a. ☐ The protected person or persons listed in item 4.

b. ☐ The residence of the protected person or persons located at (address):

c. ☐ The place of work of the protected person or persons located at (address):

d. ☐ The protected person's or persons' vehicle (specify):

e. ☐ Other (specify):

9. ☐ **ADDITIONAL ORDERS** (specify):

10. ☐ Fees for service of this order by law enforcement are waived.

11. A copy of this order and any proof of service shall be given to the additional law enforcement agencies below by the protected person or the protected person's attorney.

Law enforcement agency   Address

Date: _____

_____
JUDGE OF THE SUPERIOR COURT

THIS ORDER IS EFFECTIVE WHEN MADE. THE LAW ENFORCEMENT AGENCY SHALL ENFORCE THE ORDER IMMEDIATELY UPON RECEIPT. IT IS ENFORCEABLE ANYWHERE IN CALIFORNIA BY ANY LAW ENFORCEMENT AGENCY THAT HAS RECEIVED THE ORDER, IS SHOWN A COPY OF THE ORDER, OR HAS VERIFIED ITS EXISTENCE ON THE CALIFORNIA LAW ENFORCEMENT TELECOMMUNICATIONS SYSTEM (CLETS). IF PROOF OR SERVICE ON THE RESTRAINED PERSON HAS NOT BEEN RECEIVED, THE LAW ENFORCEMENT AGENCY SHALL ADVISE THE RESTRAINED PERSON OF THE TERMS OF THE ORDER AND THEN SHALL ENFORCE IT.

Violation of this order is a misdemeanor, punishable by a $1,000 fine, one year in jail, or both, or may be punishable as a felony. This order shall be enforced by all law enforcement officers in the State of California. Any person subject to a restraining order is prohibited from obtaining or attempting to obtain or purchase a firearm by Penal Code section 12021. Such conduct may be a felony and punishable by a $1,000 fine and imprisonment.

[SEAL]	**CLERK'S CERTIFICATE**
	I certify that the foregoing *Restraining Order After Hearing (CLETS)* is a true and correct copy of the original on file in the court.
	Date: _____ Clerk, by _____, Deputy

RESTRAINING ORDER AFTER HEARING
(Elder or Dependent Adult Abuse) (CLETS)

Document 36

Form EA-130 (Rev. Jan. 1, 2001) p. 2

The Judicial Council revised the elder abuse restraining order Form EA-130 (*Restraining Order After Hearing*) on January 1, 2001, one (1) year after the California Legislature enacted Senate Bill 218, Penal Code Section 12021(g)(3), and Family Code Section 6389(f) on January 1, 2000.

The Notice Regarding Enforcement Of This Order on page 2 of this revision violated due process and the notice requirements of amended Family Code Section 6389(f) and Penal Code Section 12021(g)(3) by failing to prohibit the respondent from *owning, possessing, purchasing, or receiving a firearm* while subjected to the protective order.

Extract from Document 36

NOTICE REGARDING ENFORCEMENT OF THIS ORDER

Violation of this order is a misdemeanor, **punishable by a $1,000 fine, one year in jail, or both. This order shall be enforced by all law enforcement officers in the State of California.**

7. ☐ **RESIDENCE EXCLUSION ORDER**
   The restrained person **must** immediately move from the residence located at the address listed in item 5a.

8. ☐ **STAY-AWAY ORDER**
   The restrained person **must** stay at least *(specify)*: _____ **yards** away from the protected person and the following places:
   a. ☐ The protected person's residence located at the address listed in item 5a.
   b. ☐ The protected person's place of work located at *(address)*:

   c. ☐ The protected person's vehicle *(specify)*:
   d. ☐ Other *(specify)*:

9. ☐ **ADDITIONAL ORDERS** *(specify)*:

10. ☐ Fees for service of this order by law enforcement are waived.

11. A copy of this order and any proof of service shall be given to the additional law enforcement agencies listed below by the protected person or the protected person's attorney.

    <u>Law enforcement agency</u>   <u>Address</u>

Date: _____   _____
                                                                                    JUDICIAL OFFICER

NOTICE REGARDING ENFORCEMENT OF THIS ORDER

This order is effective when made. The law enforcement agency shall enforce the order immediately upon receipt. It is enforceable anywhere in California by any law enforcement agency that has received the order, is shown a copy of the order, or has verified its existence on the California Law Enforcement Telecommunications System (CLETS). If proof of service on the restrained person has not been received, the law enforcement agency shall advise the restrained person of the terms of the order and then shall enforce it.

Violation of this order is a misdemeanor, punishable by a $1,000 fine, one year in jail, or both. This order shall be enforced by all law enforcement officers in the state of California.

[SEAL]	**CLERK'S CERTIFICATE**
	I certify that the foregoing *Restraining Order After Hearing (Elder or Dependent Adult Abuse) (CLETS)* is a true and correct copy of the original on file in the court.
	Date: _____ Clerk, by _____, Deputy

Document 37

Form EA-130 (Rev. July 1, 2004) p. 3

The Judicial Council revised the elder abuse post-hearing restraining order Form EA-130 (*Restraining Order After Hearing*) again on July 1, 2004, four (4) years after the California Legislature enacted Senate Bill 218, Penal Code Section 12021(g)(3), and Family Code Section 6389(f) on January 1, 2000.

The Notice Regarding Firearms on page 3 of this revision conformed to the notice requirements of amended Family Code Section 6389(f) and Penal Code Section 12021(g)(3) by prohibiting the restraining order respondent from *owning, possessing, purchasing, or receiving, or attempting to purchase or receive a firearm* while subjected to the order.

Extract from Document 37

NOTICE REGARDING FIREARMS

Unless the abuse in this case is solely financial abuse unaccompanied by force, threat, harassment, intimidation, or other form of abuse, the restrained person is ***prohibited from owning, possessing, purchasing, or receiving, or attempting to purchase or receive any firearm.* Such conduct is subject to a $1,000 fine and imprisonment.**

PETITIONER:	CASE NUMBER:
RESPONDENT:	

NOTICE REGARDING ENFORCEMENT OF THIS ORDER

This order is effective when made. The law enforcement agency shall enforce the order immediately upon receipt. It is enforceable anywhere in California by any law enforcement agency that has received the order, is shown a copy of the order, or has verified its existence on the California Law Enforcement Telecommunications System (CLETS). If proof of service on the restrained person has not been received, the law enforcement agency shall advise the restrained person of the terms of the order and then shall enforce it.

Violation of this order is a misdemeanor, punishable by a $1,000 fine, one year in jail, or both. This order shall be enforced by all law enforcement officers in the state of California.

NOTICE REGARDING FIREARMS

Unless the abuse in this case is solely financial abuse unaccompanied by force, threat, harassment, intimidation, or any other form of abuse, the restrained person is prohibited from owning, possessing, purchasing, or receiving, or attempting to purchase or receive any firearm. Such conduct is subject to a $1,000 fine and imprisonment.

[SEAL]

CLERK'S CERTIFICATE

I certify that the foregoing *Restraining Order After Hearing (Elder or Dependent Adult Abuse) (CLETS)* is a true and correct copy of the original on file in the court.

Date: Clerk, by _____, Deputy

Document 38

Form JV-250 (Rev. Jan. 1, 2000) p. 2

The Judicial Council revised the juvenile violence restraining order Form JV-250 (*Restraining Order–Juvenile*) on January 1, 2000, the same day the California Legislature enacted Senate Bill 218, Penal Code Section 12021(g)(3), and Family Code Sections 6389(c) and 6389(f).

The Firearm Restriction on page 2 of this revision violated due process and the notice requirements of the newly amended Family Code Section 6389(c) by ordering the respondents to *give up any firearm* in their *possession or control* before they had an opportunity to appear and be heard at a noticed hearing in open court, and by failing to refer to the presence or absence of the respondent at that noticed court hearing.

The violations notice in this revision also violated due process and the notice requirements of the newly amended Family Code Section 6389(f) and Penal Code Section 12021(g)(3) by failing to prohibit the restraining order respondent from *owning, possessing, purchasing, or receiving a firearm* while subjected to the protective order.

Extract from Document 38

6. FIREARM RESTRICTION
The restrained person is ordered to *give up any firearm* in or subject to his or her immediate *possession or control* within
***24 hours after issuance* of this order**
***48 hours after service* of this order**
other (*specify*)

Violations Any person subject to a restraining order is prohibited from *purchasing or attempting to purchase, receiving or attempting to receive, or otherwise obtaining a firearm*. Such conduct is subject to a $1,000 fine and imprisonment.

CASE NAME:	CASE NUMBER:

4. c. (2) *(Continued)*

           (c) ☐ The children's school or place of child care *(address optional)*:

           (d) ☐ Other *(specify)*:
           (address optional):

    d. ☐ **shall have the right to visit the minor children** named in item 2 as follows:
      (1) ☐ none   (2) ☐ visitation with the following restrictions *(specify)*:

    e. ☐ **shall NOT remove the minor children** named in item 2 from
      ☐ the State of California   ☐ other *(specify)*:

    without order of the court or other condition *(specify)*:

5. The juvenile court ☐ has ☐ has not terminated **jurisdiction** over the minor children named in item 2.

6. ☐ **FIREARM RESTRICTION**
    The restrained person is ordered to give up any firearm in or subject to his or her immediate possession or control within
    ☐ 24 hours after issuance of this order
    ☐ 48 hours after service of this order
    ☐ other *(specify)*:

    Any firearms should be surrendered to the control of local law enforcement. **The restrained person shall file a receipt with the court showing compliance with this order within 72 hours of receiving this order.**

7. **Other orders** *(specify)*:

☐ **TO THE PERSON RESTRAINED UNDER A TEMPORARY ORDER**

A court hearing has been set at the time and place indicated below. You may attend this hearing, with or without an attorney to provide any legal reason why the orders above should not be extended. If you do not appear at this hearing, the court may extend or modify the orders for up to one year without further notice to you. Upon termination of the matter by the juvenile court, the orders may be extended for up to three years.

Date: Time: Dept: Room:

Date:

                                      JUDICIAL OFFICER OF THE SUPERIOR COURT

This order is effective when made. It is enforceable in all 50 states, the District of Columbia, all tribal lands, and all U.S. territories and shall be enforced, as if it were an order of that jurisdiction, by any law enforcement agency that has received the order, is shown a copy of the order, or has verified its existence on the California Law Enforcement Telecommunications System (CLETS). If proof of service on the restrained person has not been received, and the restrained person was not present at the court hearing, the law enforcement agency shall advise the restrained person of the terms of the order and then shall enforce it.

This order meets all Full Faith and Credit requirements of the Violence Against Women Act, 18 U.S.C. 2265 (1994) (VAWA). This court has jurisdiction of the parties and the subject matter; the restrained person has been afforded notice and timely opportunity to be heard as provided by the laws of this jurisdiction.

Violations: Any person subject to a restraining order is prohibited from purchasing or attempting to purchase, receiving or attempting to receive, or otherwise obtaining a firearm. Such conduct is subject to a $1,000 fine and imprisonment. Under federal law, the issuance of a restraining order after hearing will generally prohibit the restrained person from owning, accepting, transporting, or possessing firearms or ammunition. A violation of this prohibition is a separate federal crime.

Violation of this restraining order may be punished as a contempt of court, a misdemeanor, punishable by one year in jail or a $1,000 fine, or both, or a felony. Taking or concealing a child in violation of this order is subject to state and federal criminal penalties.

(Continued on page three)

Document 39

Form JV-250 (Rev. Jan. 1, 2003) p. 2

The Judicial Council revised the juvenile violence restraining order Form JV-250 (*Restraining Order–Juvenile*) on January 1, 2003, three (3) years after the enactment of Senate Bill 218 and Family Code Section 6389(c) on January 1, 2000.

The Firearm Restriction notice on page 2 of this revision conformed to the notice requirements of amended Family Code Section 6389(c) by referring to the presence or the absence of the restraining order respondent at a prior noticed court hearing with two parenthetical phrases: *If restrained person is present at court hearing* and *If restrained person is not present at court hearing.*

Extract from Document 39

8. FIREARM RESTRICTION (mandatory after noticed hearing)
The restrained person is ordered to give up any firearm in or subject to his or her immediate possession or control within
a. 24 hours after issuance of this order (*If restrained person is present at court hearing*)
b. 48 hours after service of this order (*If restrained person is not present at court hearing*)
c. other (specify)

5. d. ☐ **must stay away at least** *(specify):* _____ yards from the following persons and places *(the addresses of these places are optional and may be kept confidential):*

    (1) ☐ **Protected persons** named in item 3

    (2) ☐ Protected person's **residence** *(address optional):*

    (3) ☐ Protected person's place of **work** *(address optional):*

    (4) ☐ The children's **school** or place of child care *(address optional):*

    (5) ☐ Protected person's **vehicle** *(description optional):*

    (6) ☐ **Other** *(specify):*

  e. ☐ **Has the right to visit the minor children** named in item 3 as follows:

    (1) ☐ none   (2) ☐ visitation according to the attached schedule (form JV-205 must be attached if any visitation is ordered)

  f. ☐ **Must NOT remove the minor children** named in item 3 from

    ☐ the State of California   ☐ other (specify):

    ☐ without order of the court or other condition (specify):

6. ☐ The child is a ward or the subject of a petition under section 601 or 602 and must not contact, threaten, stalk, or disturb the peace of *(list names):*

7. The juvenile court ☐ has ☐ has not terminated **jurisdiction** over the minor children named in item 3.

8. ☐ **FIREARM RESTRICTION** (mandatory after a noticed hearing)

The restrained person is ordered to give up any firearm in or subject to his or her immediate possession or control within

  a. ☐ 24 hours after issuance of this order. (If restrained person is present at court hearing.)

  b. ☐ 48 hours after service of this order. (If restrained person is not present at court hearing.)

  c. ☐ other *(specify):*

Any firearms should be surrendered to the control of local law enforcement or to a licensed gun dealer. **The restrained person must provide the court with a receipt or with form DV-800/JV-252 (Proof of Firearms Turned in or Sold) showing compliance with this order within 72 hours of receiving this order.**

9. **Other orders** *(specify):*

☐ **TO THE PERSON RESTRAINED UNDER A TEMPORARY ORDER**

A court hearing has been set at the time and place indicated below. You may attend this hearing, with or without an attorney, to provide any legal reason that the orders above should not be extended. If you do not appear at this hearing, the court may extend or modify the orders for up to three years without further notice to you.

Date:	Time:	Dept:	Room:

Date: _____

                                              _____

                                              JUDICIAL OFFICER

Document 40

Form JV-250 (Rev. Jan. 1, 2003) p. 3

The Judicial Council revised the juvenile violence restraining order Form JV-250 (*Restraining Order–Juvenile*) on January 1, 2003, three (3) years after the enactment of Senate Bill 218, Penal Code Section 12021(g)(3), and Family Code Section 6389(f).

The violations notice on page 3 of this revision conformed to the notice requirements of amended Family Code Section 6389(f) and Penal Code Section 12021(g)(3) by prohibiting the restraining order respondent from *owning, purchasing or attempting to purchase, receiving or attempting to receive, or otherwise obtaining a firearm.*

Extract from Document 40

Violations Any person subject to a restraining order issued after a noticed hearing is prohibited from *owning, purchasing or attempting to purchase, receiving or attempting to receive, or otherwise obtaining a firearm.* Such conduct is subject to a $1,000 fine and imprisonment. Under federal law, the issuance of a restraining order after hearing will generally prohibit the restrained person from owning, accepting, transporting, or possessing firearms or ammunition. A violation of this prohibition is a separate federal crime.

CASE NAME:	CASE NUMBERS
	JUVENILE:
	FAMILY:

This order is effective when made. It is enforceable in all 50 states, the District of Columbia, all tribal lands, and all U.S. territories and shall be enforced as if it were an order of that jurisdiction by any law enforcement agency that has received the order, is shown a copy of the order, or has verified its existence on the California Law Enforcement Telecommunications System (CLETS). If proof of service on the restrained person has not been received, and the restrained person was not present at the court hearing, the law enforcement agency shall advise the restrained person of the terms of the order and then shall enforce it.

Violations: Any person subject to a restraining order issued after a noticed hearing is prohibited from owning, purchasing or attempting to purchase, receiving or attempting to receive, or otherwise obtaining a firearm. Such conduct is subject to a $1,000 fine and imprisonment. Under federal law, the issuance of a restraining order after hearing will generally prohibit the restrained person from owning, accepting, transporting, or possessing firearms or ammunition. A violation of this prohibition is a separate federal crime.

Violation of this restraining order may be punished as a contempt of court, a misdemeanor punishable by one year in jail or a $1,000 fine, or both, or a felony. Taking or concealing a child in violation of this order is subject to state and federal criminal penalties.

Certificate of Compliance With VAWA for Temporary Orders

This temporary protective order meets all Full Faith and Credit requirements of Violence Against Women Act, 18 U.S.C 2265 (1994)(VAWA) upon notice of the restrained person. This court has jurisdiction over the parties and the subject matter; the restrained person has been or will be afforded notice and a timely opportunity to be heard as provided by the laws of this jurisdiction. **This order is valid and entitled to enforcement in all jurisdictions throughout the 50 United States, the District of Columbia, all tribal lands, and all U.S. territories, commonwealths, and possessions and shall be enforced as if it were an order of that jurisdiction.**

Certificate of Compliance With VAWA for Orders After Hearing

This protective order meets all Full Faith and Credit requirements of Violence Against Women Act, 18 U.S.C 2265 (1994) (VAWA). This court has jurisdiction over the parties and the subject matter; the restrained person has been afforded reasonable notice and an opportunity to be heard as provided by the laws of this jurisdiction. **This order is valid and entitled to enforcement in all jurisdictions throughout the 50 United States, the District of Columbia, all tribal lands, and all U.S. territories, commonwealths, and possessions and shall be enforced as if it were an order of that jurisdiction.**

CLERK'S CERTIFICATE

[SEAL]

I certify that the foregoing *Restraining Order—Juvenile (CLETS)* is a true and correct copy of the original on file in the court.

Date: _____ Clerk, by _____ , Deputy

Document 41

Form TH-110 (New July 1, 1992) p. 1

The Judicial Council republished the July 1, 1992 edition of the transitional housing restraining order Form TH-110 (*Order to Show Cause and Temporary Restraining Order*) on January 1, 2000, the same day the Legislature enacted Senate Bill 218, Penal Code Section 12021(g)(3), and Family Code Section 6389(f).

The Notice to Participant on page 1 of this republished form violated due process and the notice requirements of the newly amended Family Code Section 6389(f) and Penal Code Section 12021(g)(3) by failing to prohibit the respondent from *owning, possessing, purchasing, or receiving a firearm.* Nevertheless, the Judicial Council repeatedly republished this void July 1, 1992 edition of the TH-110, and the Courts continued to issue restraining orders on this void form for at least the seven (7) years prior to Jan. 1, 2007.

Extract from Document 41

NOTICE TO PARTICIPANT *Violation of this temporary restraining order is a misdemeanor,* **punishable by a $1,000 fine, six months in jail, or both. This order shall be enforced by all law enforcement officers in the State of California.**

ATTORNEY OR PARTY WITHOUT ATTORNEY *(Name and Address)*:	TELEPHONE NO.:	FOR COURT USE ONLY
ATTORNEY FOR *(Name)*:		

SUPERIOR COURT OF CALIFORNIA, COUNTY OF

STREET ADDRESS:

MAILING ADDRESS:

CITY AND ZIP CODE:

BRANCH NAME:

PROGRAM OPERATOR:

PARTICIPANT:

ORDER TO SHOW CAUSE ☐ and Temporary Restraining Order	CASE NUMBER:

THIS ORDER SHALL EXPIRE AT THE DATE AND THE TIME OF THE HEARING SHOWN IN THE BOX BELOW UNLESS EXTENDED BY THE COURT.

To Participant *(name all persons to be restrained or excluded)*:

YOU ARE ORDERED to appear in this court at the date, time, and place shown in the box below to give any legal reason why the orders requested in the attached petition should not be granted.

NOTICE OF HEARING

Date:	Time:	Dept.:	Room:

• *You have the right to attend the court hearing and oppose the petition, with or without an attorney.*

• *You have the right to file a response (form TH-120, copy attached) with the court without paying a fee.*

• *If you do not attend the court hearing, the court may make restraining orders against you that will last up to one year.*

> *You may obtain legal services by calling the following office:*
> *(Name of local legal services office)*:
> *(Address and telephone No.)*:

TEMPORARY RESTRAINING ORDER ☐ Not requested ☐ Denied ☐ Granted as follows:

THE COURT FINDS

1. Before the court can hold a hearing on the petition, great and irreparable harm would result to

    a. ☐ program operator

    b. ☐ program employees or their property

    c. ☐ other program participants or their property

    d. ☐ persons living within 100 feet of the program site or their property.

2. Participant

    a. ☐ **has not** been under contract with the program for more than six months *(date of contract)*:

    b. ☐ **has** been under contract with the program for more than six months, but

        (1) ☐ a restraining order is in effect and subject to further orders.

        (2) ☐ an action is pending against participant.

> **NOTICE TO PARTICIPANT:** *Violation of this temporary restraining order is a misdemeanor, punishable by a $1,000 fine, six months in jail, or both. This order shall be enforced by all law enforcement officers in the State of California.*

(Temporary Restraining Order continued on reverse)   **Page one of three**

Form Adopted by the
Judicial Council of California
TH-110 [New July 1, 1992]
Mandatory Form
WEST GROUP
ORDER TO SHOW CAUSE AND TEMPORARY RESTRAINING ORDER
(Transitional Housing Misconduct)
Health and Safety Code, § 50585

105

Document 42

Form TH-130 (New July 1, 1992) p. 1

The Judicial Council republished the July 1, 1992 edition of the transitional housing post-hearing restraining order Form TH-130 (*Order After Hearing*) on January 1, 2000, the same day the California Legislature enacted Senate Bill 218, Penal Code Section 12021(g)(3), and Family Code Section 6389(f).

The Notice to Participant on page 1 of this republished form violated due process and the notice requirements of the newly amended Family Code Section 6389(f) and Penal Code Section 12021(g)(3) by failing to prohibit the respondent from *owning, possessing, purchasing, or receiving a firearm.* Nevertheless, the Judicial Council repeatedly republished this void July 1, 1992 edition of the TH-130, and the Courts continued to issue restraining orders on this void form for at least the seven (7) years prior to January 1, 2007.

Extract from Document 42

NOTICE TO PARTICIPANT *Violation of this order is a misdemeanor,* **punishable by a $1,000 fine, six months in jail, or both. This order shall be enforced by all law enforcement officers in the State of California.**

ATTORNEY OR PARTY WITHOUT ATTORNEY *(Name and Address)*:	TELEPHONE NO.:	FOR COURT USE ONLY

ATTORNEY FOR *(Name)*:

SUPERIOR COURT OF CALIFORNIA, COUNTY OF

STREET ADDRESS:

MAILING ADDRESS:

CITY AND ZIP CODE:

BRANCH NAME:

PROGRAM OPERATOR:

PARTICIPANT:

ORDER AFTER HEARING on Petition For Order Prohibiting Abuse or Program Misconduct ☐ **Modification of Previous Order** *(dated)*:	CASE NUMBER:

NOTE: *A separate order is required for each participant or family unit to be restrained or excluded.*

To participant *(names of all to be restrained or excluded)*:

1. THIS ORDER SHALL EXPIRE AT MIDNIGHT ON *(date not more than one year from now)*:

2. This proceeding was heard
   on *(date)*:   at *(time)*:   in Dept.:   Room:
   by Judge *(name)*:   ☐ Temporary Judge
   on the order to show cause filed by program operator on *(date)*:
   ☐ Program operator present   ☐ Attorney for operator present *(name)*:
   ☐ Participant present *(names)*:
   ☐ Attorney for participant present *(name)*:

> **NOTICE TO PARTICIPANT:** *Violation of this order is a misdemeanor, punishable by a $1,000 fine, six months in jail, or both. This order shall be enforced by all law enforcement officers in the State of California.*

THE COURT ORDERS

3. ☐ **Program misconduct.** Participant shall not intentionally violate the program rules and regulations so as to interfere substantially with the orderly operation of the program and specifically the rules and regulations on
   a. ☐ drunkenness on the program site *(rule No.)*:
   b. ☐ unlawful use or sale of controlled substances (drugs) *(rule No.)*:
   c. ☐ theft *(rule No.)*:
   d. ☐ arson *(rule No.)*:
   e. ☐ destruction of property *(rule No.)*:
   f. ☐ violence or threats of violence and harassment *(rule No.)*:

4. ☐ **Do not abuse.** Participant shall not attack, strike, batter, or sexually assault, or threaten to attack, strike, batter, or sexually assaul
   a. ☐ program employees
   b. ☐ program participants
   c. ☐ persons living within 100 feet of the program site
   ☐ and specifically the following persons *(names)*:

(Continued on reverse)

Form Adopted by the
Judicial Council of California
TH-130 [New July 1, 1992]
Mandatory Form

ORDER AFTER HEARING
(Transitional Housing Misconduct)

WEST GROUP   Health and Safety Code, § 50585

Document 43

Form WV-120 (New Jan. 1, 2000) p. 3

The Judicial Council published a new Workplace Violence restraining order Form WV-120 (*Order to Show Cause and Temporary Restraining Order*) on January 1, 2000, the same day the California Legislature enacted Senate Bill 218, Penal Code Section 12021(g)(3), and Family Code Section 6389(f).

The violations notice on page 1 of this new form violated due process and the notice requirements of the newly amended Family Code Section 6389(f) and Penal Code Section 12021(g)(3) by failing to prohibit the restraining order respondent from *owning, possessing, purchasing, or receiving a firearm* while subjected to the protective order.

Extract from Document 43

Violation of this order is a misdemeanor, punishable by a $1,000 fine, one year in jail, or both, or may be punishable as a felony. This order shall be enforced by all law enforcement officers in the State of California. Any person subject to a restraining order is prohibited from *obtaining or purchasing or attempting to obtain or purchase a firearm* by Penal Code section 12021. Such conduct may be a felony and punishable by a $1,000 fine and imprisonment.

PLAINTIFF (Name):	CASE NUMBER:
DEFENDANT (Name):	

TEMPORARY RESTRAINING ORDER

Violation of this order is a misdemeanor, punishable by a $1,000 fine, one year in jail, or both, or may be punishable as a felony. This order shall be enforced by all law enforcement officers in the State of California. Any person subject to a restraining order is prohibited from obtaining or purchasing or attempting to obtain or purchase a firearm by Penal Code section 12021. Such conduct may be a felony and punishable by a $1,000 fine and imprisonment.

THE COURT FINDS

5. a. The defendant is (name):

> Sex: ☐ M ☐ F Ht.: ____ Wt.: ____ Hair color: ____ Eye color: ____ Race: ____ Age: ____ Date of birth: _____

b. The protected employee is (name):

c. Protected family or household members who reside with employee are:

(1) **(Name)**:

> Sex: ☐ M ☐ F Date of birth: _____

(2) **(Name)**:

> Sex: ☐ M ☐ F Date of birth: _____

(3) **(Name)**:

> Sex: ☐ M ☐ F Date of birth: _____ ☐ Continued on Attachment 5c.

UNTIL THE TIME OF HEARING, IT IS ORDERED

6. **Defendant** is prohibited from further violence or threats of violence against protected person.
   and SPECIFICALLY IT IS ORDERED THAT DEFENDANT
   a. ☐ shall not assault, batter, or stalk the employee and other protected persons
   b. ☐ shall not follow or stalk the employee and other protected persons to or from the place of work
   c. ☐ shall not follow the employee and other protected persons during hours of employment
   d. ☐ shall not telephone or send correspondence to the employee and other protected persons by **any** means including, but not limited to, the use of the public or private mails, interoffice mail, fax, or computer e-mail
   e. ☐ shall not enter the workplace of the employee and other protected persons
   f. ☐ other (specify):

7. ☐ Defendant is ordered to stay at least (specify): _____ yards away from the following persons and places (the addresses of the places are optional and may be kept confidential):
   a. ☐ Employee and other protected persons (names):

   b. ☐ Residence of employee and other protected persons (address optional):

   c. ☐ Place of work of employee and other protected persons (address optional):

(Continued on reverse)

WV-120 [New January 1, 2000]

**ORDER TO SHOW CAUSE AND
TEMPORARY RESTRAINING ORDER (CLETS)
(Workplace Violence)**

Page three of four

109

Document 44

Form WV-120 (Rev. Jan. 1, 2003) p. 4

The Judicial Council revised the workplace violence restraining order Form WV-120 (*Order to Show Cause and Temporary Restraining Order*) on January 1, 2003, three (3) years after the California Legislature enacted Senate Bill 218, Penal Code Section 12021(g)(3), and Family Code Sections 6389(c) and 6389(f) on January 1, 2000.

The Mandatory Firearm Relinquishment notice on page 4 of this revision conformed to the notice requirements of amended Family Code Section 6389(c) by referring to the presence or the absence of the restraining order respondent at a prior noticed court hearing with two parenthetical phrases: *If restrained person is present at hearing* and *If restrained person is not present at hearing.*

The Notice Regarding Firearms in this 2003 revision also conformed to the notice requirements of amended Family Code Section 6389(f) and Penal Code Section 12021(g)(3) by prohibiting the respondent from *owning, possessing, purchasing or attempting to purchase, receiving or attempting to receive, or otherwise obtaining a firearm.*

Extract from Document 44

10. MANDATORY FIREARM RELINQUISHMENT

The restrained person must surrender to local law enforcement or sell to a licensed gun dealer any firearm in or subject to his or her immediate possession or control within

a. 24 hours after issuance of this order (*If restrained person is present at court hearing*)

b. 48 hours after service of this order (*If restrained person is not present at court hearing*)

NOTICE REGARDING FIREARMS

Any person subject to a restraining order is prohibited from *owning, possessing, purchasing or attempting to purchase, receiving or attempting to receive, or otherwise obtaining a firearm*. Such conduct is subject to a $1,000 fine and imprisonment.

PLAINTIFF (Name):	CASE NUMBER:
DEFENDANT (Name):	

9. ☐ OTHER ORDERS (specify):

10. **MANDATORY FIREARM RELINQUISHMENT**
    The restrained person must surrender to local law enforcement or sell to a licensed gun dealer any firearm in or subject to his or her immediate possession or control within
    a. ☐ 24 hours after issuance of this order (if restrained person is present at hearing).
    b. ☐ 24 hours after service of this order (if restrained person is not present at hearing).
    c. ☐ other (specify):

    The restrained person shall file a receipt with the court showing compliance with this order within 72 hours of receiving this order.

11. ☐ Application for an order shortening time is granted and the following documents shall be personally served on the defendant no less than (specify number):   days before the time set for hearing:
    a. *Order to Show Cause and Temporary Restraining Order (CLETS) (Workplace Violence)* (form WV-120)
    b. *Petition of Employer for Injunction Prohibiting Violence or Threats of Violence Against Employee (Workplace Violence)* (WV-100)
    c. blank *Response to Petition of Employer for Injunction Prohibiting Violence or Threats of Violence Against Employee (Workplace Violence)* (WV-110)
    d. blank *Proof of Service of Completed Response* (form WV-131)
    e. other (specify):

12. By the close of business on the date of this order, a copy of this order and any proof of service shall be given to the law enforcement agencies listed below as follows:
    a. ☐ Plaintiff shall deliver.
    b. ☐ Plaintiff's attorney shall deliver.

    Law enforcement agency   Address

Date:

_____
JUDICIAL OFFICER
☐ SIGNATURE FOLLOWS LAST ATTACHMENT

This order is effective when made. It is enforceable anywhere in all 50 states, the District of Columbia, all tribal lands, and all U.S. territories and shall be enforced as if it were an order of that jurisdiction by any law enforcement agency that has received the order, is shown a copy of the order, or has verified its existence on the California Law Enforcement Telecommunications System (CLETS). If proof of service on the restrained person has not been received, and the restrained person was not present at the court hearing, the law enforcement agency shall advise the restrained person of the terms of the order and then shall enforce it. Violations of this restraining order are subject to criminal penalties.

NOTICE REGARDING FIREARMS
Any person subject to a restraining order is prohibited from owning, possessing, purchasing or attempting to purchase, receiving or attempting to receive, or otherwise obtaining a firearm. Such conduct is subject to a $1,000 fine and imprisonment.

WV-120 [Rev. January 1, 2003]   **ORDER TO SHOW CAUSE AND TEMPORARY RESTRAINING ORDER (CLETS)**   Page 4 of 4
(Workplace Violence)

Document 45

Form WV-140 (New Jan. 1, 2000) p. 1

The Judicial Council published a new workplace violence restraining order Form WV-140 (*Order After Hearing on Petition of Employer for Injunction Prohibiting Violence or Threats of Violence Against Employee*) on January 1, 2000, the same day the Legislature enacted Senate Bill 218, Penal Code Section 12021(g)(3), and Family Code Section 6389(f).

The violations notice on page 1 of this new form violated due process and the notice requirements of the newly amended Family Code Section 6389(f) and Penal Code Section 12021(g)(3) by failing to prohibit the restraining order respondent from *owning, possessing, purchasing, or receiving a firearm* while subjected to the protective order.

Extract from Document 45

Violation of this order is a misdemeanor, punishable by a $1,000 fine, one year in jail, or both, or may be punishable as a felony. This order shall be enforced by all law enforcement officers in the State of California. Any person subject to a restraining order is prohibited from *obtaining or purchasing or attempting to obtain or purchase a firearm* by Penal Code section 12021. Such conduct may be a felony and punishable by a $1,000 fine and imprisonment.

ATTORNEY OR PARTY WITHOUT ATTORNEY *(Name, state bar number, and address)*:	FOR COURT USE ONLY
TELEPHONE NO.: FAX NO.:	
ATTORNEY FOR *(Name)*:	
NAME OF COURT:	
STREET ADDRESS:	
MAILING ADDRESS:	
CITY AND ZIP CODE:	
BRANCH NAME:	
PLAINTIFF:	
DEFENDANT:	
EMPLOYEE:	

ORDER AFTER HEARING ON PETITION OF EMPLOYER FOR INJUNCTION PROHIBITING VIOLENCE OR THREATS OF VIOLENCE AGAINST EMPLOYEE (CLETS)	CASE NUMBER:

1. THIS ORDER SHALL EXPIRE AT MIDNIGHT ON *(date)*:
2. This proceeding came on for hearing as follows:

Date:	Time:	Dept.:	Room:

3. Judge *(name)*:   ☐ Temporary judge
4. a. ☐ Plaintiff present   ☐ Attorney present *(name)*:
   b. ☐ Defendant present   ☐ Attorney present *(name)*:

THE COURT FINDS

5. a. The defendant is *(name)*:

   Sex: ☐ M ☐ F Ht.: ____ Wt.: ____ Hair color: ____ Eye color: ____ Race: ____ Age: ____ Date of birth: ____

   b. The protected employee is *(name)*:

   Sex: ☐ M ☐ F Date of birth: _____

   c. Protected family or household members who reside with employee are:
   (1) *(Name)*:

   Sex: ☐ M ☐ F Date of birth: _____

   (2) *(Name)*:

   Sex: ☐ M ☐ F Date of birth: _____

   (3) *(Name)*:

   Sex: ☐ M ☐ F Date of birth: _____   ☐ Continued on Attachment 5c.

Violation of this order is a misdemeanor, punishable by a $1,000 fine, one year in jail, or both, or may be punishable as a felony. This order shall be enforced by all law enforcement officers in the State of California. Any person subject to a restraining order is prohibited from obtaining or purchasing or attempting to obtain or purchase a firearm by Penal Code section 12021. Such conduct may be a felony and punishable by a $1,000 fine and imprisonment.

(Continued on reverse)

Form Approved for Optional Use
Judicial Council of California
WV-140 [New January 1, 2000]

ORDER AFTER HEARING ON PETITION OF EMPLOYER FOR INJUNCTION PROHIBITING VIOLENCE OR THREATS OF VIOLENCE AGAINST EMPLOYEE (CLETS)
(Workplace Violence)

WEST GROUP

Code of Civil Procedure, § 527.8;
Penal Code, § 273.6(a)

Document 46

Form WV-140 (Rev. Jan. 1, 2003) p. 3

The Judicial Council revised the workplace violence restraining order Form WV-140 (*Order After Hearing on Petition of Employer for Injunction Prohibiting Violence or Threats of Violence Against Employee*) on January 1, 2003, three (3) years after the California Legislature enacted Senate Bill 218, Penal Code Section 12021(g)(3), and Family Code Section 6389(f) on January 1, 2000.

The Notice Regarding Firearms on page 3 of this revision conformed to the notice requirements of amended Family Code Section 6389(f) and Penal Code Section 12021(g)(3) by prohibiting the respondent from *owning, possessing, purchasing or attempting to purchase, receiving or attempting to receive, or otherwise obtaining a firearm.*

Extract from Document 46

NOTICE REGARDING FIREARMS

Any person subject to a restraining order is prohibited from *owning, possessing, purchasing or attempting to purchase, receiving or attempting to receive, or otherwise obtaining a firearm.* Such conduct is subject to a $1,000 fine and imprisonment.

PLAINTIFF (Name):	CASE NUMBER:
DEFENDANT (Name):	

10. By the close of business on the date of this order, a copy of this order and any proof of service shall be given to the law enforcement agencies listed below as follows:

a. ☐ Plaintiff shall deliver.

b. ☐ Plaintiff's attorney shall deliver.

           Law enforcement agency   Address

This order is effective when made. It is enforceable anywhere in all 50 states, the District of Columbia, all tribal lands, and all U.S. territories and shall be enforced as if it were an order of that jurisdiction by any law enforcement agency that has received the order, is shown a copy of the order, or has verified its existence on the California Law Enforcement Telecommunications System (CLETS). If proof of service on the restrained person has not been received, and the restrained person was not present at the court hearing, the law enforcement agency shall advise the restrained person of the terms of the order and then shall enforce it. Violations of this restraining order are subject to criminal penalties.

NOTICE REGARDING FIREARMS

Any person subject to a restraining order is prohibited from owning, possessing, purchasing or attempting to purchase, receiving or attempting to receive, or otherwise obtaining a firearm. Such conduct is subject to a $1,000 fine and imprisonment.

Date: _____

_____
JUDICIAL OFFICER

**ORDER AFTER HEARING ON PETITION OF EMPLOYER
FOR INJUNCTION PROHIBITING VIOLENCE
OR THREATS OF VIOLENCE AGAINST EMPLOYEE (CLETS)
(Workplace Violence)**

Epilogue
A Voided Generation

The documents in this book reveal the misunderstanding and obvious confusion pervading the Judicial Council's belated response to the enactment of Senate Bill 218. These documents also reveal the Council's decisions on April 28, 2000 and October 27, 2000 to revise the Firearm Restriction notice and the Notice Regarding Firearms in the DV-110, DV-130, and MC-220 to conform to Constitutional and statutory law. They also illustrate the inevitable and tragic consequences this generation of void restraining order forms had on a generation of young men from California's minority communities.

On January 1, 1999 the Judicial Council published three (3) restraining order forms that violated the prior notice and due process guarantees of the California and U.S. Constitutions. Then, on January 1, 2000 the Council republished these three restraining order forms, plus (8) more restraining order forms, all of which violated the firearms notice requirements of the newly enacted Senate Bill 218. Shortly thereafter, on April 1, 2000, the Council published two (2) more forms that also violated the requirements of Senate Bill 218, bringing the total number of void and unenforceable California restraining order forms to thirteen (13).

The Judicial Council failed until July 1, 2000 to conform any of the state's restraining order forms to the statutory requirements of amended Family Code Section 6389(f) and Penal Code Section 12021(g)(3) by including a warning notice that prohibited respondents from *owning, possessing, purchasing, or receiving a firearm.* The Council also decided against publishing a one-page warning notice the Courts could have attached to the appropriate void forms to make the forms valid because *attaching the warning to every restraining order might be burdensome to court clerks and individuals.*

Additionally, the Judicial Council failed until January 1, 2001 to revise the Firearm Restriction in the DV-110 and the DV-130 to conform to amended Family Code Section 6389(c) by referring to a prior *noticed hearing,* and the Council failed to revise the MC-220 to conform to the requirements of Senate Bill 218 for six (6) years, until the form was finally dropped from the commercial forms books on January 1, 2007. Nor did the Council manage to revise the state's other restraining order forms until three (3) to more than four and a half (4.5) years after the enactment of Senate Bill 218.

There is no doubt these publishing mistakes occurred as set forth in this book, because the public record demonstrates that by July 1, 2004 the Judicial Council had eventually managed to revise the majority, though not all, of the state's restraining order forms to conform to the requirements of Senate Bill 218. But the public record also shows that none of the state's restraining order forms were conformed to the new law until a year after the Legislature's January 1, 2000 deadline, and that the Council was still supplying the California Courts with void and unenforceable restraining order forms as late as January 1, 2007.

There is also no doubt that while these void restraining orders were wreaking havoc on the state's minority population, the Judicial Council was quietly revising the same forms without a word to anyone other than their judicial colleagues. Apparently nobody gave a thought to telling the affected petitioners and respondents, their legal representatives, or anyone in the public or the press that the Council's publishing mistakes had voided every California restraining order as of January 1, 2000.

Nor does anyone on the Judicial Council or in the AOC seem to have cared that the Council's conclusion that *attaching the warning to every restraining order might be burdensome to court clerks and individuals* and the Council's subsequent decision to forgo publishing an alternative form would compel the California Courts to issue a whole generation of void and unenforceable restraining orders on void Judicial Council forms. Or that this generation of void restraining orders would falsely imprison and void the lives of a whole generation of presumably innocent respondents without the warning notice or prior hearing required by state and federal due process guarantees and the new Senate Bill 218.

Appendices

Appendix A

List of Void Restraining Orders
January 1, 1999–January 1, 2007

List of Void Forms with Year Published and Year Conformed

Form No.	Form Name	Published	Conformed	Yrs. Void
1295.90/ EPO-001	Emergency Protective Order	Rev. Jan. 1, 2000	Rev. Jan. 1, 2004	3
CH-120	Order to Show Cause & TRO	Rev. Jan. 1, 1999	Rev. Jan. 1, 2003	3
CH-140	Order After Hearing	Rev. Jan. 1, 1999	Rev. Jan. 1, 2003	3
DV-110	Order to Show Cause & TRO	New Jan. 1, 1999	Rev. Jan. 1, 2001	2
DV-130	Order After Hearing	New Jan. 1, 1999	Rev. Jan. 1, 2001	2
EA-120	Order to Show Cause & TRO	New April 1, 2000	Rev. July 1, 2004	4.25
EA-130	Order After Hearing	New April 1, 2000	Rev. July 1, 2004	4.25
JV-250	Restraining Order-Juvenile	Rev. Jan. 1, 2000	Rev. Jan. 1, 2003	3
MC-220	Order in Criminal Proceeding	Rev. Jan. 1, 1999	Dropped Jan. 1, 2007	8
TH-110	Order to Show Cause & TRO	New July 1, 1992	Never conformed	7 plus
TH-130	Order After Hearing	New July 1, 1992	Never conformed	7 plus
WV-120	Order to Show Cause & TRO	New Jan. 1, 2000	Rev. Jan. 1, 2003	3
WV-140	Order After Hearing	New Jan. 1, 2000	Rev. Jan. 1, 2003	3

Appendix B

Table of Void Restraining Orders
January 1, 1999–January 1, 2007

Key: **No**=Void
     Yes=Valid
     N/A=Not Available

Forms by Number and Years Void

Form No.	Form Name	Jan 99	Jul 99	Jan 00	Jul 00	Jan 01	Jul 01	Jan 02	Jul 02	Jan 03	Jul 03	Jan 04	Jul 04	Jan 05	Jul 05	Jan 06	Jul 06
1295.90/EPO-001	Emergency Protective Order	Yes	Yes	No	No	No	No	No	No	Yes	Yes	Yes	Yes	Yes	Yes	Yes	Yes
CH-120	Order to Show Cause and TRO	Yes	Yes	No	No	No	No	No	No	Yes	Yes	Yes	Yes	Yes	Yes	Yes	Yes
CH-140	Order After Hearing	Yes	Yes	No	No	No	No	No	No	Yes	Yes	Yes	Yes	Yes	Yes	Yes	Yes
DV-110	Order to Show Cause and TRO	No	No	No	No	Yes	Yes	Yes	Yes	Yes	Yes	Yes	Yes	Yes	Yes	Yes	Yes
DV-130	Order After Hearing	No	No	No	No	Yes	Yes	Yes	Yes	Yes	Yes	Yes	Yes	Yes	Yes	Yes	Yes
EA-120	Order to Show Cause and TRO	N/A	N/A	N/A	No	No	No	No	No	No	No	No	Yes	Yes	Yes	Yes	Yes
EA-130	Order After Hearing	N/A	N/A	N/A	No	No	No	No	No	No	No	No	Yes	Yes	Yes	Yes	Yes
JV-250	Restraining Order-Juvenile	Yes	Yes	No	No	No	No	No	No	No	Yes	Yes	Yes	Yes	Yes	Yes	Yes
MC-220	Order in Criminal Proceeding	No	No	No	No	No	No	No	No	No	No	No	No	No	No	No	No
TH-110	Order to Show Cause and TRO	Yes	Yes	No	No	No	No	No	No	No	No	No	No	No	No	No	No
TH-130	Order After Hearing	Yes	Yes	No	No	No	No	No	No	No	No	No	No	No	No	No	No
WV-120	Order to Show Cause and TRO	Yes	Yes	No	No	No	No	No	No	Yes	Yes	Yes	Yes	Yes	Yes	Yes	Yes
WV-140	Order After Hearing	Yes	Yes	No	No	No	No	No	No	Yes	Yes	Yes	Yes	Yes	Yes	Yes	Yes

Appendix C

The UCLA Research Study (June 6, 2003)

Three years after the enactment of Senate Bill 218, three researchers from the School of Public Health at UCLA conducted a study of the active restraining orders listed in California's Domestic Violence Restraining Order System as of June 6, 2003.

The goal of this study was to accurately determine the class of persons most frequently ordered to be restrained, the usual restrained and protected person pairings, and the conditions contained in the printed restraining orders themselves. This study placed particular emphasis on the presence or absence of firearms restrictions in the restraining order forms.

Pertinent findings from this study are shown in the extracted quotes below.

Extract from UCLA Study

Findings There were 227,941 restraining orders in the statewide database against adults on June 6, 2003. In 72.2% of the orders a woman was to be protected and a man was to be restrained. In 19.3%, the restrained person and the protected person were of the same sex. Mutual restraining orders were rare. Rates of restraining orders (i.e., restrained persons) were highest for *men* (1,496.6 per 100,000), *25-34 year olds* (1,366.8 per 100,000), and *Blacks* (2,437.5 per 100,000). About *one tenth* of the restraining orders listed *no firearms prohibitions*. Moreover, *one in six restraining orders were never served*, so even fewer were aware of the restrictions that were imposed.

Extracted from:

Restraining orders in California A look at 227,941 prohibited purchasers, By Susan B. Sorensen, Haikang Shen, and Katherine A. Vittes, U.C.L.A. School of Public Health, U.C.L.A., 650 C.E. Young Drive South, Los Angeles, CA 90095-1772, June 6, 2003.

PUBLIC HEALTH
AND THE ENVIRONMENT
November 6-10, 2004 · Washington, DC

APHA

Restraining orders in California: A look at 227,941 prohibited purchasers

Susan B. Sorenson, PhD, Haikang Shen, PhD, and **Katherine A. Vittes, MPH**. School of Public Health, UCLA, 650 C.E. Young Drive South, Los Angeles, CA 90095-1772, 310-825-8749, kavittes@ucla.edu

Background. Each year, the largest new class of persons who are prohibited by law from purchasing a firearm are those against whom a restraining order has been issued. This research tabulates statewide administrative data for all types of restraining orders to describe persons ordered to be restrained, the restrained and protected person pairing, and conditions of the order itself, with particular emphasis on firearms restrictions.

Method. All restraining orders listed in California's Domestic Violence Restraining Order System on June 6, 2003 constituted the study population. Descriptive statistics were calculated.

Findings. There were 227,941 restraining orders in the statewide database against adults on June 6, 2003. In 72.2% of the orders a woman was to be protected and a man was to be restrained. In 19.3%, the restrained person and the protected person were of the same sex. Mutual restraining orders were rare. Rates of restraining orders (i.e., restrained persons) were highest for men (1,496.6 per 100,000), 25-34 year olds (1,366.8 per 100,000), and Blacks (2,437.5 per 100,000). About one tenth of the restraining orders listed no firearms prohibitions. Moreover, one in six restraining orders were never served, so even fewer were aware of the restrictions that were imposed.

Conclusions. In California, there are as many restraining orders active on a given day as there are marriages during one year. Suggestions are made for how forms could be constructed and how restraining orders are served as well as about the logistics of implementing aspects of relevant laws.

Learning Objectives: At the conclusion of this session, participants will be able to

- describe firearms restrictions associated with restraining orders;
- describe demographic groups at highest risk of having a restraining order issued against them;
- recognize how restraining order processes can be improved, with a particular focus on associated firearms restrictions.

Presenting author's disclosure statement:
I do not have any significant financial interest/arrangement or affiliation with any organization/institution whose products or services are being discussed in this session.

Sports and Firearms Poster Session

The 132nd Annual Meeting (November 6-10, 2004) of APHA

The DOJ Report (July 2002) p. 11

In July of 2002 the Criminal Justice Statistics Center for the California Department of Justice (DOJ) reported the results of a statewide study of the number of people arrested in 1998, 1999, and 2000 for allegedly violating Penal Code Sections 12021 or 12021.1 by *owning or possessing a firearm.*

As shown on the next page, the study found that in 1999, when the forms DV-110, DV-130, and MC-220 were Constitutionally void, a total of *5,919* people were arrested for allegedly violating Penal Code Sections 12021 or 12021.1. Another *6,219* people were arrested in 2000 for allegedly violating these same Penal Code sections, after every California Judicial Council restraining order form was voided by the enactment of Senate Bill 218 and Penal Code Section 12021(g)(3) on January 1, 2000.

Extracted from

Special Report to the Legislature on Senate Bill 1608: Arrests and court dispositions of felons and others arrested for firearms possession in California's 58 counties. **By Bill Lockyer, Attorney General, California Department of Justice, Division of California Justice Information Services, Bureau of Criminal Information and Analysis, Criminal Justice Statistics Center, July 2002.**

Table 1
Arrests in 1998-2000 for PC Sections 12021 or 12021.1
By County

County	Total			Number of arrests for violations of PC Sections 12021 or 12021.1 (only)			Number of arrests for violations of PC Sections 12021 or 12021.1 (with other law violations)		
	1998	1999	2000	1998	1999	2000	1998	1999	2000
Statewide total	6,657	5,919	6,219	2,369	1,844	1,739	4,288	4,075	4,480
Alameda	497	444	349	192	184	142	305	260	207
Alpine	1	0	0	1	0	0	0	0	0
Amador	10	6	11	7	3	2	3	3	9
Butte	81	68	56	28	18	18	53	50	38
Calaveras	7	11	9	2	3	3	5	8	6
Colusa	13	6	4	2	2	0	11	4	4
Contra Costa	216	197	231	54	65	52	162	132	179
Del Norte	10	6	4	3	0	1	7	6	3
El Dorado	41	28	14	11	9	2	30	19	12
Fresno	128	117	158	21	18	32	107	99	126
Glenn	10	13	10	3	2	2	7	11	8
Humboldt	28	24	23	11	4	6	17	20	17
Imperial	16	23	18	5	9	5	11	14	13
Inyo	3	5	10	1	2	3	2	3	7
Kern	209	214	209	21	31	15	188	183	194
Kings	14	8	15	5	3	5	9	5	10
Lake	26	18	22	7	6	6	19	12	16
Lassen	21	4	3	11	2	1	10	2	2
Los Angeles	1,245	1,181	1,381	942	650	645	303	531	736
Madera	39	16	32	7	6	9	32	10	23
Marin	8	14	11	4	4	3	4	10	8
Mariposa	14	6	5	6	2	2	8	4	3
Mendocino	50	42	47	12	9	5	38	33	42
Merced	45	40	56	8	11	8	37	29	48
Modoc	2	6	2	0	0	0	2	6	2
Mono	1	1	4	1	1	1	0	0	3
Monterey	122	101	113	25	30	23	97	71	90
Napa	20	12	21	6	1	5	14	11	16
Nevada	20	25	16	6	9	4	14	16	12
Orange	385	326	359	91	83	69	294	243	290
Placer	34	33	40	10	12	8	24	21	32
Plumas	5	5	3	3	2	0	2	3	3
Riverside	321	358	337	125	98	104	196	260	233
Sacramento	371	295	416	115	39	63	256	256	353
San Benito	1	4	7	0	1	0	1	3	7
San Bernardino	610	544	533	212	194	146	398	350	387
San Diego	446	340	394	77	63	79	369	277	315
San Francisco	194	190	215	21	20	23	173	170	192
San Joaquin	180	157	146	28	27	38	152	130	108
San Luis Obispo	23	21	16	5	5	2	18	16	14
San Mateo	72	91	73	13	16	13	59	75	60
Santa Barbara	41	33	27	9	6	11	32	27	16
Santa Clara	311	247	222	41	28	25	270	219	197
Santa Cruz	42	25	33	10	7	11	32	18	22
Shasta	60	32	46	9	5	11	51	27	35
Sierra	0	1	2	0	1	1	0	0	1
Siskiyou	19	22	17	5	7	6	14	15	11
Solano	140	95	93	28	16	17	112	79	76
Sonoma	94	72	81	30	13	13	64	59	68
Stanislaus	141	138	97	30	31	17	111	107	80
Sutter	18	9	18	6	2	5	12	7	13
Tehama	20	29	18	10	5	5	10	24	13
Trinity	11	8	4	4	3	0	7	5	4
Tulare	64	53	51	47	35	32	17	18	19
Tuolumne	19	25	21	3	9	5	16	16	16
Ventura	52	54	57	15	12	20	37	42	37
Yolo	51	38	39	11	9	10	40	29	29
Yuba	29	27	16	7	7	3	22	20	13
Unknown county	6	11	4	2	4	2	4	7	2

11

Appendix E
Senate Bill 218 (April 26, 1999) Sec. 5

SEC. 5. Section 6389 of the Family Code is amended to read.

6389. (a) A person subject to a protective order, as defined in Section 6218, shall not own, possess, purchase, or receive a firearm while that protective order is in effect.

(b) The Judicial Council shall provide a notice on all forms requesting a protective order that, at the hearing for a protective order, the respondent shall be ordered to relinquish possession or control of any firearms and not to purchase or receive or attempt to purchase or receive any firearms for a period not to exceed the duration of the restraining order.

(c) If the respondent is present in court at a duly noticed hearing, the court shall order the respondent to relinquish any firearm in that person's immediate possession or control, or subject to that person's immediate possession or control, within 24 hours of the order, by either surrendering the firearm to the control of local law enforcement officials, or by selling the firearm to a licensed gun dealer, as specified in Section 12071 of the Penal Code. *If the respondent is not present at the hearing, the respondent shall relinquish the firearm within 48 hours after being served with the order.* A person ordered to relinquish any firearm pursuant to this subdivision shall file with the court a receipt showing the firearm was surrendered to the local law enforcement agency or sold to a licensed gun dealer within 72 hours after receiving the order. In the event that it is necessary to continue the date of any hearing due to a request for a relinquishment order pursuant to this section, the court shall ensure that all applicable protective orders described in Section 6218 remain in effect or bifurcate the issues and grant the permanent restraining order pending the date of the hearing.

(d) If the respondent declines to relinquish possession of any firearm based upon the assertion of the right against self-incrimination, as provided by the Fifth Amendment to the United States Constitution and Section 15 of Article I of the California Constitution, the court may grant use immunity for the act of relinquishing the firearm required under this section.

(e) A local law enforcement agency may charge the respondent a fee for the storage of any firearm pursuant to this section. This fee shall not exceed the actual cost incurred by the local law enforcement agency for the storage of the firearm. For purposes of this subdivision, "actual cost" means expenses directly related to taking possession of a firearm, storing the firearm, and surrendering possession of the firearm to a licensed dealer as defined in Section 12071 of the Penal Code or to the respondent.

(f) The restraining order requiring a person to relinquish a firearm pursuant to subdivision (c) shall state on its face that the respondent is prohibited from owning, possessing, purchasing, or receiving a firearm while the protective order is in effect and that the firearm shall be relinquished to the local law enforcement agency for that jurisdiction or sold to a licensed gun dealer, and that proof of surrender or sale shall be filed with the court within a specified period of receipt of the order. The order shall also state on its face the expiration date for relinquishment. Nothing in this section shall limit a respondent's right under existing law to petition the court at a later date for modification of the order.

(g) The restraining order requiring a person to relinquish a firearm pursuant to subdivision (c) shall prohibit the person from possessing or controlling any firearm for the duration of the order. At the expiration of the order, the local law enforcement agency shall return possession of any surrendered firearm to the respondent, within five days after the expiration of the relinquishment order, unless the local law enforcement agency determines that (1) the firearm has been stolen, (2) the respondent is prohibited from possessing a firearm because the respondent is in any prohibited class for the possession of firearms, as defined in Sections 12021 and 12021.1 of the Penal Code and Sections 8100 and 8103 of the Welfare and Institutions Code, or (3) another successive restraining order is used against the respondent under this section. If the local law enforcement agency determines that the respondent is the legal owner of any firearm deposited with the local law enforcement agency and is prohibited from possessing any firearm, the respondent shall be entitled to sell or transfer the firearm to a licensed dealer as defined in Section 12071 of the Penal Code. If the firearm has been stolen, the firearm shall be restored to the lawful owner upon his or her identification of the firearm and proof of ownership.

(h) The court may, as part of the relinquishment order, grant an exemption from the relinquishment requirements of this section for a particular firearm if the respondent can show that a particular firearm is necessary as a condition of continued employment and that the current employer is unable to reassign the respondent to another position where a firearm is unnecessary. If an exemption is granted pursuant to this subdivision, the order shall provide that the firearm shall be in the physical possession of the respondent only during scheduled work hours and

127

during travel to and from his or her place of employment. In any case involving a peace officer who as a condition of employment and whose personal safety depends on the ability to carry a firearm, a court may allow the peace officer to continue to carry a firearm, either on duty or off duty, if the court finds by a preponderance of the evidence that the officer does not pose a threat of harm. Prior to making this finding, the court shall require a mandatory psychological evaluation of the peace officer and may require the peace officer to enter into counseling or other remedial treatment program to deal with any propensity for domestic violence.

(i) During the period of the relinquishment order, a respondent is entitled to make one sale of all firearms that are in the possession of a local law enforcement agency pursuant to this section. A licensed gun dealer, who presents a local law enforcement agency with a bill of sale indicating that all firearms owned by the respondent that are in the possession of the local law enforcement agency have been sold by the respondent to the licensed gun dealer, shall be given possession of those firearms, at the location where a respondent's firearms are stored, within five days of presenting the local law enforcement agency with a bill of sale.

(j) The disposition of any unclaimed property under this section shall be made pursuant to Section 1413 of the Penal Code.

(k) The return of a firearm to any person pursuant to subdivision (g) shall not be subject to the requirements of subdivision (d) of Section 12072 of the Penal Code.

(l) If the respondent notifies the court that he or she owns a firearm that is not in his or her immediate possession, the court may limit the order to exclude that firearm if the judge is satisfied the respondent is unable to gain access to that firearm while the protective order is in effect.

(m) Any respondent to a protective order who violates any order issued pursuant to this section shall be punished under the provisions of subdivision (g) of Section 12021 of the Penal Code.

Appendix F
Senate Bill 218 (April 26, 1999) Sec. 17

SEC. 17. Section 12021 of the Penal Code is amended to read

12021. (a) (1) Any person who has been convicted of a felony under the laws of the United States, of the State of California, or any other state, government, or country, or of an offense enumerated in subdivision (a), (b), or (d) of Section 12001.6, or who is addicted to the use of any narcotic drug, who owns or has in his or her possession or under his or her custody or control any firearm is guilty of a felony.

(2) Any person who has two or more convictions for violating paragraph (2) of subdivision (a) of Section 417 and who owns or has in his or her possession or under his or her custody or control any firearm is guilty of a felony.

(b) Notwithstanding subdivision (a), any person who has been convicted of a felony or of an offense enumerated in Section 12001.6, when that conviction results from certification by the juvenile court for prosecution as an adult in an adult court under Section 707 of the Welfare and Institutions Code, who owns or has in his or her possession or under his or her custody or control any firearm is guilty of a felony.

(c) (1) Except as provided in subdivision (a) or paragraph (2) of this subdivision, any person who has been convicted of a misdemeanor violation of Section 71, 76, 136.5, or 140, subdivision (d) of Section 148, Section 171b, 171c, 171d, 186.28, 240, 241, 242, 243, 244.5, 245, 245.5, 246, 246.3, 247, 273.5, 273.6, 417, 417.1, 417.2, 417.6, 626.9, 646.9, 12023, or 12024, subdivision (b) or (d) of Section 12034, Section 12040, subdivision (b) of Section 12072, subdivision (a) of former Section 12100, Section 12220, 12320, or 12590, or Section 8100, 8101, or 8103 of the Welfare and Institutions Code, any firearm-related offense pursuant to Sections 871.5 and 1001.5 of the Welfare and Institutions Code, or of the conduct punished in paragraph (3) of subdivision (g) of Section 12072, and who, within 10 years of the conviction, owns, or has in his or her possession or under his or her custody or control, any firearm is guilty of a public offense, which shall be punishable by imprisonment in a county jail not exceeding one year or in the state prison, by a fine not exceeding one thousand dollars ($1,000), or by both that imprisonment and fine. The court, on forms prescribed by the Department of Justice, shall notify the department of persons subject to this subdivision. However, the prohibition in this paragraph may be reduced, eliminated, or conditioned as provided in paragraph (2) or (3).

(2) Any person employed as a peace officer described in Section 830.1, 830.2, 830.31, 830.32, 830.33, or 830.5 whose employment or livelihood is dependent on

the ability to legally possess a firearm, who is subject to the prohibition imposed by this subdivision because of a conviction under Section 273.5, 273.6, or 646.9, may petition the court only once for relief from this prohibition. The petition shall be filed with the court in which the petitioner was sentenced. If possible, the matter shall be heard before the same judge that sentenced the petitioner. Upon filing the petition, the clerk of the court shall set the hearing date and shall notify the petitioner and the prosecuting attorney of the date of the hearing. Upon making each of the following findings, the court may reduce or eliminate the prohibition, impose conditions on reduction or elimination of the prohibition, or otherwise grant relief from the prohibition as the court deems appropriate

(A) Finds by a preponderance of the evidence that the petitioner is likely to use a firearm in a safe and lawful manner.

(B) Finds that the petitioner is not within a prohibited class as specified in subdivision (a), (b), (d), (e), or (g) or Section 12021.1, and the court is not presented with any credible evidence that the petitioner is a person described in Section 8100 or 8103 of the Welfare and Institutions Code.

(C) Finds that the petitioner does not have a previous conviction under this subdivision no matter when the prior conviction occurred. In making its decision, the court shall consider the petitioner's continued employment, the interest of justice, any relevant evidence, and the totality of the circumstances. The court shall require, as a condition of granting relief from the prohibition under this section, that the petitioner agree to participate in counseling as deemed appropriate by the court. Relief from the prohibition shall not relieve any other person or entity from any liability that might otherwise be imposed. It is the intent of the Legislature that courts exercise broad discretion in fashioning appropriate relief under this paragraph in cases in which relief is warranted. However, nothing in this paragraph shall be construed to require courts to grant relief to any particular petitioner. It is the intent of the Legislature to permit persons who were convicted of an offense specified in Section 273.5, 273.6, or 646.9 to seek relief from the prohibition imposed by this subdivision.

(3) Any person who is subject to the prohibition imposed by this subdivision because of a conviction of an offense prior to that offense being added to paragraph (1), may petition the court only once for relief from this prohibition. The petition shall be filed with the court in which the petitioner was sentenced. If possible, the matter shall be heard before the same judge that sentenced the petitioner. Upon filing the petition, the clerk of the court shall set the hearing date and notify the

petitioner and the prosecuting attorney of the date of the hearing. Upon making each of the following findings, the court may reduce or eliminate the prohibition, impose conditions on reduction or elimination of the prohibition, or otherwise grant relief from the prohibition as the court deems appropriate.

(A) Finds by a preponderance of the evidence that the petitioner is likely to use a firearm in a safe and lawful manner.

(B) Finds that the petitioner is not within a prohibited class as specified in subdivision (a), (b), (d), (e), or (g) or Section 12021.1, and the court is not presented with any credible evidence that the petitioner is a person described in Section 8100 or 8103 of the Welfare and Institutions Code.

(C) Finds that the petitioner does not have a previous conviction under this subdivision, no matter when the prior conviction occurred. In making its decision, the court may consider the interest of justice, any relevant evidence, and the totality of the circumstances. It is the intent of the Legislature that courts exercise broad discretion in fashioning appropriate relief under this paragraph in cases in which relief is warranted. However, nothing in this paragraph shall be construed to require courts to grant relief to any particular petitioner.

(4) Law enforcement officials who enforce the prohibition specified in this subdivision against a person who has been granted relief pursuant to paragraph (2) or (3), shall be immune from any liability for false arrest arising from the enforcement of this subdivision unless the person has in his or her possession a certified copy of the court order that granted the person relief from the prohibition. This immunity from liability shall not relieve any person or entity from any other liability that might otherwise be imposed.

(d) Any person who, as an express condition of probation, is prohibited or restricted from owning, possessing, controlling, receiving, or purchasing a firearm and who owns, or has in his or her possession or under his or her custody or control, any firearm but who is not subject to subdivision (a) or (c) is guilty of a public offense, which shall be punishable by imprisonment in a county jail not exceeding one year or in the state prison, by a fine not exceeding one thousand dollars ($1,000), or by both that imprisonment and fine. The court, on forms provided by the Department of Justice, shall notify the department of persons subject to this subdivision. The notice shall include a copy of the order of probation and a copy of any minute order or abstract reflecting the order and conditions of probation.

(e) Any person who (1) is alleged to have committed an offense listed in subdivision

(b) of Section 707 of the Welfare and Institutions Code, an offense described in subdivision (b) of Section 1203.073, or any offense enumerated in paragraph (1) of subdivision (c), and (2) is subsequently adjudged a ward of the juvenile court within the meaning of Section 602 of the Welfare and Institutions Code because the person committed an offense listed in subdivision (b) of Section 707 of the Welfare and Institutions Code, an offense described in subdivision (b) of Section 1203.073, or any offense enumerated in paragraph (1) of subdivision (c) shall not own, or have in his or her possession or under his or her custody or control, any firearm until the age of 30 years. A violation of this subdivision shall be punishable by imprisonment in a county jail not exceeding one year or in the state prison, by a fine not exceeding one thousand dollars ($1,000), or by both that imprisonment and fine. The juvenile court, on forms prescribed by the Department of Justice, shall notify the department of persons subject to this subdivision. Notwithstanding any other law, the forms required to be submitted to the department pursuant to this subdivision may be used to determine eligibility to acquire a firearm.

(f) Subdivision (a) shall not apply to a person who has been convicted of a felony under the laws of the United States unless either of the following criteria is satisfied

(1) Conviction of a like offense under California law can only result in imposition of felony punishment.

(2) The defendant was sentenced to a federal correctional facility for more than 30 days, or received a fine of more than one thousand dollars ($1,000), or received both punishments.

(g)(1) Every person who purchases or receives, or attempts to purchase or receive, a firearm knowing that he or she is subject to a protective order as defined in Section 6218 of the Family Code, Section 136.2, or a temporary restraining order or injunction issued pursuant to Section 527.6 or 527.8 of the Code of Civil Procedure, is guilty of a public offense, which shall be punishable by imprisonment in a county jail not exceeding one year or in the state prison, by a fine not exceeding one thousand dollars ($1,000), or by both that imprisonment and fine. This subdivision does not apply unless the copy of the restraining order personally served on the person against whom the restraining order is issued contains a notice in bold print stating (1) that the person is prohibited from purchasing or receiving or attempting to purchase or receive a firearm and (2) specifying the penalties for violating this subdivision, or a court has provided actual verbal notice of the firearm prohibition and penalty as provided in Section 6304 of the Family Code.

(2) Every person who owns or possesses a firearm knowing that he or she is prohibited from owning or possessing a firearm by the provisions of a protective order as defined in Section 6218 of the Family Code, Section 136.2 of the Penal Code, or a temporary restraining order or injunction issued pursuant to Section 527.6 or 527.8 of the Code of Civil Procedure, is guilty of a public offense, which shall be punishable by imprisonment in a county jail not exceeding one year, by a fine not exceeding one thousand dollars ($1,000), or by both that imprisonment and fine. *This subdivision does not apply unless a copy of the restraining order personally served on the person against whom the restraining order is issued contains a notice in bold print stating (1) that the person is prohibited from owning or possessing or attempting to own or possess a firearm and (2) specifying the penalties for violating this subdivision, or a court has provided actual verbal notice of the firearm prohibition and penalty as provided in Section 6304 of the Family Code.*

(3) Judicial Council shall provide notice on all protective orders that the respondent is prohibited from owning, possessing, purchasing, or receiving a firearm while the protective order is in effect and that the firearm shall be relinquished to the local law enforcement agency for that jurisdiction or sold to a licensed gun dealer, and that proof of surrender or sale shall be filed within a specified time of receipt of the order. The order shall also state on its face the expiration date for relinquishment.

(4) If probation is granted upon conviction of a violation of this subdivision, the court shall impose probation consistent with the provisions of Section 1203.097.

(h) (1) A violation of subdivision (b), (c), (d), or (e) is justifiable where all of the following conditions are met

(A) The person found the firearm or took the firearm from a person who was committing a crime against him or her.

(B) The person possessed the firearm no longer than was necessary to deliver or transport the firearm to a law enforcement agency for that agency's disposition according to law.

(C) If the firearm was transported to a law enforcement agency, it was transported in accordance with paragraph (18) of subdivision (a) of Section 12026.2.

(D) If the firearm is being transported to a law enforcement agency, the person transporting the firearm has given prior notice to the law enforcement agency that he or she is transporting the firearm to the law enforcement agency for disposition according to law.

(2) Upon the trial for violating subdivision (a), (b), (c), (d), or (e), the trier of fact shall determine whether the defendant was acting within the provisions of the exemption created by this subdivision.

(3) The defendant has the burden of proving by a preponderance of the evidence that he or she comes within the provisions of the exemption created by this subdivision.

Appendix G

Void Orders and the Common Law

Klugh v. United States

A void order or judgment is one which, from its inception is and forever continues to be absolutely null, without legal efficacy, ineffectual to bind parties or support a right, of no legal force and effect whatever, and incapable of confirmation, ratification, or enforcement in any manner or to any degree. Judgment is a "void judgment" if the court that rendered judgment lacked jurisdiction of the subject matter, or of the parties, or acted in a manner inconsistent with due process [*Klugh v. United States*, D.C.S.C., 620 F.Supp. 892, 901].

Shank/Balfour Beatty v. I.B.E.W. Local 99

Although denial of a motion for relief from judgment or order is normally reviewed for abuse of discretion, district court has no discretion when deciding motion to vacate judgment as void because judgment is either void or it is not [*Shank/Balfour Beatty, a Joint Venture of M.L. Shank Co., Inc., Balfour Beatty Construction, Inc. v. International Brotherhood of Electrical Workers Local 99*, C.A.1 (R.I.) (2007) 497 F.3d 83].

V.T.A., Inc. v. Airco, Inc.

If judgment is void, it is necessary to evaluate the validity of the underlying judgment in reviewing an order denying a motion for relief from judgment and, if the underlying judgment is void, an order based on it is void; if voidness is found, relief is not discretionary but is mandatory [*V.T.A. Inc. v. Airco, Inc.* CA10 (Colo.) (1979) 597 F.2d 220].(2007) 497 F.3d 83].

Elliot v. Piersol

If a court is without authority, its judgments and orders are regarded as nullities. They are not voidable, but simply void; and form no bar to a recovery sought, even prior to a reversal in opposition to them. They constitute no justification; and all persons concerned in executing such judgments or sentences, are considered, in law, as trespassers [*Elliot v. Piersol* (1828) (1 Pet. 328, 340)].

Fritts v. Krugh

A 'void' judgment, as we all know, grounds no rights, forms no defense to actions taken thereunder, and is vulnerable to any manner of collateral attack (thus here, by habeas corpus). No statute of limitations or repose runs on its holdings, the matters thought to be settled thereby are not res judicata, and years later, when the memories may have grown dim and rights long been regarded as vested, any disgruntled litigant may reopen old wounds and once more probe their depths. And it is then as though trial and adjudication had never been [*Fritts v. Krugh*, S. Ct. of Michigan (1958) 92 N.W.2d 604].

About the Author

The author is a former law office manager turned freelance legal researcher, with over twenty years of experience with the California Judicial Council's mandatory legal forms.

Notes

Notes

Notes

www.ingramcontent.com/pod-product-compliance
Lightning Source LLC
Chambersburg PA
CBHW081647270326
41933CB00018B/3377